FOR CRYING OUT LOUD

FOR CRYING OUT LOUD

CONNECTING THROUGH GRIEF AND LOSS IN A DIGITAL ERA

LEA ZIKMUND

NEW DEGREE PRESS

COPYRIGHT © 2022 LEA ZIKMUND

All rights reserved.

FOR CRYING OUT LOUD

Connecting Through Grief and Loss in a Digital Era

ISBN	979-8-88504-576-6	*Paperback*
	979-8-88504-920-7	*Kindle Ebook*
	979-8-88504-692-3	*Ebook*

CONTENTS

INTRODUCTION		7
PART ONE		**15**
CHAPTER 1.	THE SLOW TEMPERATURE CHANGE	17
CHAPTER 2.	CAN WE STOP PERFORMING?	27
CHAPTER 3.	OVERSHARING, OVERSHAMING	37
CHAPTER 4.	"HANDLING IT": INDIVIDUALISM AS THE ANTITHESIS TO COMMUNITY	47
CHAPTER 5.	ALGORITHMS AND USER EXPERIENCES	57
CHAPTER 6.	FINDING COMMUNITY	67
CHAPTER 7.	WHEN WE HONOR THE LOVE, WE HONOR OURSELVES	79
CHAPTER 8.	HUMAN FIRST, PROFESSIONAL SECOND	89
CHAPTER 9.	SOCIAL MEDIA AS MODERN DAY MOURNING GEAR	97
CHAPTER 10.	BECOMING THE SPECTACLE: WHAT WE CAN LEARN FROM INTERACTING WITH GRIEF	107

PART TWO		**117**
	INTRODUCTION: A GRIEVER'S UTOPIA	119
CHAPTER 11.	INFLUENCER THERAPIST	123
CHAPTER 12.	GRIEFCHAT	133
CHAPTER 13.	INFLUENCER COACHES	149
CHAPTER 14.	@GOTTHEGRANDPAGENE	161
CHAPTER 15.	THE ROOM	171
	CONCLUSION	177
	ACKNOWLEDGMENTS	181
	APPENDIX	185

INTRODUCTION

In September 2020, I opened Instagram and saw a photo of Chrissy Teigen sitting on a hospital bed, hands clasped in front of her face and her shoulders bare as she leaned over crying. The black-and-white photo's caption states, "We are shocked and in the kind of deep pain you only hear about, the kind of pain we've never felt before. We were never able to stop the bleeding and give our baby the fluids he needed, despite bags and bags of blood transfusions. It just wasn't enough."

I read and reread her post. I scrolled through comments that sent support to her and her family. Later that night, I talked about the post with a friend. We both pushed back tears over how often this happens and how important it was that she shared it.

In the coming weeks, after Chrissy Teigen posted about losing her pregnancy, I realized this story took a front row seat in popular media outlets. Among people like myself, who were grateful she shared her story, were others, who felt it was inappropriate. Sportswriter and culture critic Jason Whitlock tweeted about Teigen's post, stating, "I don't understand this or social media. Who takes pictures of their deepest pain and then shares it with strangers?" Almost a month after the original post, Teigen released a Medium article about the post and her experience losing Jack, who was to be her third child. In it, she stated:

> "I cannot express how little I care that you hate the photos. How little I care that it's something you wouldn't have done. I lived it, I chose to do it, and more than anything, these photos aren't for anyone but the people who have lived this or are curious enough to wonder what something like this is like. These photos are only for the people who need them. The thoughts of others do not matter to me."

Engaging with this moment was one of the many catalysts for my interest in how we share and interpret the pain of others in social media spaces. I thought of how unsurprising it was that a personal moment, once shared, became controversial. I started to wonder when the idea of sharing was associated with negativity and if this is something we can learn from.

Social media's prevalence in our current society is hardly news. Some might say we should get rid of it entirely—and maybe they have a point. But unless there's some sort of technological glitch that completely shuts down every platform through which we share our lives, this seems unlikely. To live with social media and see it as a tool, like other tools we were previously equipped with, seems like a better option to me.

According to an October 2021 study published by Backlinko, over 60 percent of the global population uses social media. In the United States, that number reaches beyond 70 percent. Globally, the average person spends about 2.5 hours on social media a day. A March 2021 article from Vox showed since the start of the COVID-19 pandemic, every social media platform has reported increased user growth as people spent more time at home, socially distanced from friends and loved ones.

Knowing that collectively, many of us use social media quite often, it seems important to focus on what exactly we share there. Is it a whole picture of our lives? What does it reflect about our culture and society at large?

Hashtags on social media help track the usage of certain terms and trends. While there are too many hashtags in existence to account for individually, prevalent ones can indicate the type of content shared today. For example, on Instagram there are currently thirty-five million posts listed under #Joy and 160 million under #Happiness. There are only two million posts under #Grief, two million under #Loss, and five million under #Death. With such significant gaps between these subjects, what can we learn?

If someone were to begin using social media for the first time today, it may appear happiness and joy are the most common experiences and emotions across the board for the majority of people. In reality, I think we can agree this is far from the truth. All of our life experiences are a blend of many emotions—hardships and joys—but we are not always invited to share the whole picture.

My belief is social media, to an extent, still remains a highlight reel, *but that this is changing.* The problem is we aren't all in agreement with the change, so posts that whisk us away from the highlight reel status quo can be jarring or confusing if we don't understand the intent. If the average person spends more than two hours a day engaging with social media, we need to start realizing social media itself is a facet of our society and our culture. What I'm hoping is that instead of scrapping it altogether, we learn how to better use social media by sharing more authentically.

For as long as I've had social media, I've observed the norms and patterns of how people share and what is mainstream, criticized, or something in between. I use social media and observe its trends, controversies, and evolution on a daily basis as your average social media user. I even convinced my college advisor to let me analyze Instagram posts for my final thesis project! But not until my dad became really sick did I start to reflect more on what *I* wanted to share about my life and what I hoped to get from the platform.

My dad spent the majority of 2020 and 2021 in and out of doctors' offices and hospital rooms. For a while, the root of the issue seemed a bit unclear. By December 2020, we learned on top of liver disease, he also had liver cancer. Hearing the C Word brought a new level of bleakness to the situation, because, unlike all the terms I had heard previously, I actually knew this one. I was so scared. Through conversations with several doctors and specialists, we were told he needed a liver transplant and would start the process of getting listed.

To say this process was overwhelming would be a major understatement. I often felt frozen, not sure what steps to take next or how to anticipate the next challenge. Living in New York at the time, I would make trips back home to Pennsylvania, when I could, if my dad needed support. Eventually, I'd return to New York after spending long days in hospitals and doctors' offices, dodging work calls and feeling overwhelmed with everything on my plate, only to realize I lived in what's often been described as the loneliest city in the country.

I was desperate for connection and to talk to people who could say, "I get it."

This is when the shift happened for me, when I realized I paid much closer attention to my friends and acquaintances who were caretakers or had recently experienced a loss. Their life experiences felt closer to mine than that of the average twenty-five year old and social media is what helped remind me my people were out there and this experience wasn't an isolated one.

Before I even conceptualized this book, I was already engaging in a day-to-day attempt at connection through social media platforms, following therapists who spoke on grief and loss, and exchanging direct messages with friends talking about their experiences. It felt good and important for me to have a sense of solidarity with people whose experiences aligned with mine. I started sharing more of my perspective, first just to close friends, but then to the wider audience of people I'm connected with on social media.

On October 1, 2021, we got the long awaited call that there was a liver available for my dad and we needed to be ready for surgery by the next morning. Through complications with the procedure and sleepless nights in a shared hotel bed with my older sister, I knew I needed to document this experience and wanted to share it as it happened.

I have never felt so connected to those in my life than in those moments of sharing. Sitting and worrying between calls from our dad's surgeon, my sister and I updated Facebook and Instagram, sharing about the complications and triumphs of the experience. I received over a hundred direct messages from close friends, acquaintances, and people I hadn't spoken to in years. They sent prayers, pictures of their pets (upon my request), and many offered to send us meals or open up their home for us to stay.

A difficult experience and a major procedure such as a liver transplant was made more positive because of my and my sister's willingness to open it up to a wider community, ask for what we needed, and allow people to offer help in whatever ways they could. Reading messages of encouragement to our dad while he spent weeks recovering in the hospital contributed to everyone's morale and continued to remind us we weren't alone.

In the back of my head, though, I'd occasionally wonder if I might be taking up too much space and if sharing so much was a horrible idea or seemed attention seeking. I worried people would have the same reaction I witnessed in Chrissy Teigen's story—if they thought I should have kept this to myself and suffer in silence, as people are often encouraged to do.

With this book, I intend to uncover some of the historical components of how social media has evolved while contextualizing it in American society. How have we learned to use these platforms and how do our cultural practices influence that use? I think by piecing these components together, we can better understand why some people are still uncomfortable with the types of sharing on social media that might actually bring us closer together.

I have interviewed friends, acquaintances, and strangers for this book, asking them all about their choices to share about their own journeys with grief and loss on social media. The big essential question is: *did it help?* Is there something about social media that can help us process these moments? Could we envision the possibility that sharing online can feel different than sharing in person? Could it be better in some ways?

As I wrote, I realized how much there is to know and understand, not just about a complex experience like grief but also about social media and how we interact with it. While there are many published numbers and statistics related to social media usage, I think the psychological impact of social networking sites is still relatively hard to measure. So, I moved into a more creative space with the work and wrote several fictional essays that are meant to get at some of the themes behind grief and loss when it comes to social media use. You will find those essays in Part 2: A Griever's Utopia—an oxymoron, I know.

I hope you will enjoy the stories, both fiction and nonfiction, that you read in this book. I hope they make you think about the platforms you use and how you interpret other people's use of them as well. While some people find social media quite trivial, my intention is to give context that will help us understand its benefits. I hope we can move forward with new ways of using and understanding these platforms as methods of leveraging connection and healing through our most difficult moments.

PART ONE

CHAPTER 1

THE SLOW TEMPERATURE CHANGE

———

On the morning of September 11, 2001, I sat on my family's beige, shaggy carpet eating a peanut butter and jelly sandwich when I saw news coverage of the attack on the Twin Towers. My dad was taking a nap on the couch after his night shift, something he often did before taking me to my afternoon kindergarten class. He always had the news on in the background when he napped. I watched the footage of the attack as it replayed again and again on the news but could not make sense of what I saw. All I knew was something terrible had happened.

On June 25, 2009, I ate dinner with my family with the news on in the background, as usual. I remember the way my mom's mood shifted from her usual cheerfulness to absolute devastation when she realized Michael Jackson had died. There was a strange, empty feeling that loomed over our house. It was as if we had lost a friend. Days following this announcement, my mom and her friend Cherré would play Michael Jackson concert DVDs in our living room on full volume and celebrate his legacy, dancing to "Thriller" and crying during "Earth Song."

In early November 2016, my friends and I sat outside a college apartment while we watched the election results come in increments through the night. I wore a sticker that said, "I voted!" for my first time participating in a presidential election. We started the evening with a feeling of hope and excitement but slowly drifted off to our separate dorm rooms and apartments. I woke up the morning of November 9 and checked Instagram to confirm the awful dream I'd had the night before—that Trump had won the election. I scrolled through my feed to see which of my friends were also sharing their feelings about the election.

By May 2020, just months into a global pandemic, many of us, on multiple social media platforms, watched a video repeatedly of a police officer murdering George Floyd outside a grocery store in Minneapolis, Minnesota. While rising tensions in the United States had already led to painful divisions, this situation created even more polarization, bringing conversations of race and policing into focus. For a short period of time, there was a wave and plethora of activism, resources, and awareness on social media.

These four events serve as smaller bookmarks and pillars of my upbringing, but I remember them specifically because of how I learned about them. The news, once merely a backdrop in the soundscape of daily life, has become a much more prevalent facet of our lives because of social media.

When the Twin Towers were attacked, my parents might have had their first cell phones, ginormous and archaic compared to today's devices. The idea of communicating information through social networking sites was not yet central to our culture. As I moved out of my teenage years and into early adulthood, I noticed more and more social media was a place where I could receive more than just social connection. These platforms also provided news articles, resources, memes, recipes, and essentially everything someone could want to know, all in one place: a one-stop shop for the human experience.

The problem is social media has evolved tremendously in a short period of time, but we have not evolved to use it much differently. Yes, there are new platforms and features, but that doesn't necessarily mean we use social media in a way that fosters stronger connection. I think we're in a social media use plateau and we need to recognize it.

The Social Dilemma is a 2020 Netflix documentary analyzing how Big Tech influences social networking. It highlights some of the biggest players in tech, such as Google and Facebook, the advances of these platforms, and how addicting they have become to the everyday user. The documentary also raises ethical concerns about the continued advancements of features that invite the daily user to engage more and more with the platforms, including features such as notifications, being tagged in photos, and the "like" button.

The Social Dilemma highlights the work of Jaron Lanier, the Silicon Valley "computer philosopher." Among his many accomplishments are coining the term "virtual reality" and creating VPL Research, the first company to sell virtual reality products. In 2018, Lanier published *Ten Arguments for Deleting Your Social Media Right Now*. For the reader's convenience, the back cover of his book lists all ten reasons, as follows:

1. You are losing your free will.
2. Quitting social media is the most finely targeted way to resist the insanity of our times.
3. Social media is making you into an asshole.
4. Social media is undermining truth.
5. Social media is making what you say meaningless.
6. Social media is destroying your capacity for empathy.
7. Social media is making you unhappy.
8. Social media doesn't want you to have economic dignity.
9. Social media is making politics impossible.
10. Social media hates your soul.

The book itself was controversial. I read many book reviews that were either vehemently against Lanier's ideas or enthusiastically in agreement. On one hand, there is truth to his arguments—undoubtedly, certain aspects of social media are heavily rooted in capitalism. On the other hand, social networking sites have become crucial spaces for people to connect and collaborate. What can we do when these tensions exist?

In response to his suggestion, I will admit deleting your social media can be helpful and keep you away from a lot of the evils people point out about social media: addiction, mindless scrolling, and manipulation by advertisements and companies—the list continues.

However, believing the deletion of our accounts will solve the ills of social media is like believing abstinence-only sex education is comprehensive and works for everyone. It may be a problem that can be solved from within if we understand the issue itself at a more nuanced degree.

I continued to dive into Lanier's work and found a 2018 TED Talk called, "How we need to remake the Internet". In it, Lanier presents a fascinating evolution of early digital culture to where we are now. He talks about the "lefty" mindset that was foundational to making the Internet accessible to all people when it first began in the 1990s. Early digital culture was formed around the idea that the Internet had to be entirely accessible to the public so as to avoid inequity. At the same time, Lanier notes the rise in tech entrepreneurs, like Steve Jobs, stood at a stark contrast to this ideology.

"How do you celebrate entrepreneurship when everything is free?" Lanier asks.

According to Lanier, the solution to this tension became the implementation of advertisements on sites like Google and Facebook. Although this idea may have started out as a seemingly innocent solution to keeping the Internet free while supporting innovative business strategies, people and companies only got better at targeting customers' likes and dislikes. Lanier notes there are now universities where people study these kinds of algorithms and how to improve their accuracy for this very purpose.

With advertisements, Lanier argues social media is no longer social media, but rather behavior modification that rewards and punishes the behavior of its users. In other words, people and companies rapidly receive feedback through social media use and continue to cater to the audiences that respond to them with both extreme praise and extreme negativity.

To fix this problem, Lanier suggests we "remake the decision" behind Internet use, arguing we should offer subscription or micropayment options for Internet use that provide higher quality options and less of the junk. I imagine he has encountered strong disagreement with this idea because he quickly mentions this is not a new conceptual model for the use of technology. Television services like Netflix and Hulu already use this model, and because of that, they operate under the basis that with small subscription fees they can offer better quality content to their users.

In contrast, Google and Facebook are really the only entities that rely on advertisements as their primary business model. This means no matter how powerful they are as companies, they still need these advertisement options in order to continue. "I don't believe our species can survive unless we fix this. We cannot have a society in which, if two people wish to communicate, the only way that can happen is if it's financed by a third person who wishes to manipulate them," Lanier says. He closes by suggesting that unless we can accomplish this new model, we should delete our social media, as he states in his book.

Lanier is a passionate, well-informed, and convincing speaker. I appreciate that he can critique the industry where he has been so successful and at the same time present the solutions that he practices. From listening to him speak, I can tell we agree on a fundamental idea:

Social media may continue to advance, but these advancements do not benefit individuals or humanity as a collective.

My issue with Lanier's work is that it does not more broadly acknowledge the fact that capitalism has a role in almost every way people connect with each other right now. If you meet a friend at a coffee shop to catch up, you are likely to buy a coffee or treat in exchange for the time you spend at the establishment. In the background, while the radio plays, you might hear advertisements to buy the next best item on the market. You leave the coffee shop and pass by someone selling T-shirts on the street. None of this is new.

There is no reason we cannot connect in humane ways simply because of the presence of capitalism on the sites where these interactions take place. In fact, it is vital we connect *more* in spite of capitalism creeping into every crevice of our society. Lanier proposes a business model that charges for certain Internet services that would not only make social networking higher quality but also invite more human interaction. He also acknowledges this would take a lot of time and effort.

What I propose is a more human interaction *with* social networking sites that can contribute to this change as well. If we show up as ourselves and see others doing the same, we might feel less inclined to constantly improve who we are and showcase something that isn't real in the first place. If we show up as ourselves, that advertisement for a new shirt or pair of sneakers is not going to have the same hold on us as it might have now.

I believe big ideas that resonate with people can spread across a community and make waves. We see it in protests, the creation of unions in workplaces, and other collective social movements. I think we need to make a shift, now, from social media to human media.

Think about how often people refer to social media as a "highlight reel." This is because it is easy for people to share joy and accomplishments on these platforms, like pregnancy announcements, promotions, new relationships, wedding photos, first home purchases—the list goes on. These sorts of things are easy to access on any social media platform, but we know it isn't the entire picture of someone's lived experience.

Most industries that fight for our attention bank on our dissatisfaction with some facet of our lives. The beauty industry is a great example of this, exacerbating people's insecurities about how they look to convince them to purchase a product. Want to reverse the effects of aging? Buy this new, expensive face cream! Feeling nervous about bathing suit season? It's not too late to join our weight loss program! This is a very visible issue, and every day I see content creators trying to reverse this narrative by normalizing parts of our bodies we are meant to feel shame about. This is effective because it begs us to confront that which makes us feel insecure in the first place, rather than hating what is natural and normal within ourselves.

Imagine we translate that same logic into our moments of grief, loss, and hardship. Why would anyone profit off those moments? Technically, they don't, but they profit off platforms that perpetuate the narrative that having certain possessions and achieving certain successes bring happiness. For someone experiencing grief or loss, there is no room to express that in a space like social media without eventually feeling like the pendulum needs to swing back to its original position.

You may be thinking to yourself grief and loss are private and not meant to be shared. What I hope we can consider is *why* these are private experiences when others are not. Why is having a baby a moment to be shared but having one and losing it is to be kept secret?

I took away a lot of wisdom from *The Social Dilemma,* including something technology ethicist Tristan Harris said. Harris's work has been fundamental to understanding the root of social networking sites' issues. He states, "It's not about the technology being the existential threat. It's the technology's ability to bring out the worst in society [...] and the worst in society being the existential threat."

To me, this is an important reminder we are not meant to be passive users of our social media. It is there for us to engage and connect and I think powerful things can happen when we use it in that way. But, just like other vices, without intention and understanding of the ways that social media can cause harm, we run into major issues.

I do not plan on deleting my social networking accounts. As you will learn in later chapters, social media has been a necessary component to my journey as a young caretaker. It is a vital resource to communities and individuals when it comes to social movements and smaller scale connective experiences. We cannot lose these connections.

It is easy not to notice a temperature change when it happens slowly over a long period of time. You realize it when it is too late, when you can hardly stand it anymore. Luckily, I believe social media is merely a tool over which we still have control. We can notice how it has changed and we can do something about it.

CHAPTER 2

CAN WE STOP PERFORMING?

"Social media is just the market's answer to a generation that demanded to perform, so the market said, 'Here, perform everything to each other all the time for no reason.' It's prison, it's horrific. It's performer and audience, melded together. What do we want more than to lie in our bed at the end of the day and just watch our life as a satisfied audience member? I know very little about anything, but what I do know is that if you can live your life without an audience, you should do it."

—BO BURNHAM, *MAKE HAPPY*.

When I analyze the slow temperature change of social media's prevalence in our society today, it is not without acknowledgment of the fact my experience with it has vast differences from those of other generations. Growing up with social media meant I slowly adapted to it as a facet of my life, while I watched people my parents' age and beyond feel frustrated they had to learn a new system and find new ways to connect with people just to keep up.

I distinctly remember in my teenage years helping my Grammy use Facebook on her iPad, which she bought to keep in touch with our many family members. Admittedly, I remember feeling frustrated because all these systems felt so natural for me to use and I couldn't understand why someone would struggle with it.

I remember first downloading Instagram and seeing most of the content there were selfies and pictures of people's latte art. Nothing was very serious or nuanced, but rather centered around a very simple photo-sharing interaction.

As things grew and changed, more pieces of our lives became part of what we shared online. Photo captions became longer and more representative of a blog-style writing form. People would include questions in their captions to invoke thoughts or comments, one of the many tactics influencers use to increase engagement. Slowly, we morphed into a use of social media that has allowed us to be with each other twenty-four seven: a day in the life of [insert career here], get ready with me videos, and videos of what people eat for breakfast, lunch, and dinner.

I think it can be damaging to constantly have access to each other all the time and compare what our lives look like in reference to a snapshot of those we see. Logically, I believe we can all recognize portrayals of others online are not a complete window into reality, but it is hard to remind yourself of this if you use social media on a regular basis.

Now more than ever I can sense people fear the harmful effects social media has on all of us.

From *The Social Dilemma*, I learned plastic surgeons have coined a new term: "snapchat dysmorphia." It refers to the increasing amount of people getting plastic surgery to replicate the filters they see on Snapchat and other social media platforms. With more virtual tools to morph our bodies and faces into unrealistic shapes, colors, and sizes, there is increased pressure to adhere to new beauty standards on social media platforms. Logically, I believe most people understand the photos they see on social media are edited and tampered with to portray perfection, but it is clear this still affects people's views of themselves.

The documentary also points out harrowing statistics about the correlation between self-harm and suicide rates and the availability of social media on mobile devices around 2009. *The Social Dilemma* notes that from 2010 to 2011, the number of hospital admissions for non-fatal self-harm for girls ages fifteen to nineteen has increased by 62 percent, and for girls ages ten to fourteen by 189 percent. Compared to statistics from 2001 to 2009, they also found suicide rates are up 70 percent for girls ages fifteen to nineteen and 151 percent for girls ages ten to fourteen.

There is a growing body of research working to understand the psychological impacts of social media use on things like self-esteem and mental health. A 2017 study published by Sage Journals took an intimate look at people's Instagram usage and how it contributes to body image, eating disorders, and general self-esteem. Among their findings was a strong correlation between time spent on social networking sites and increased dieting.

"[Social networking sites] create an environment with multiple social comparisons, often made to somewhat idealized images, as users are likely to post only photographs showing themselves *looking good* or *doing something cool*," the study comments.

I worry about the impact of performing a perfect life for others, but more so about the pressure people feel to perform that life for *themselves*. While the idea of feigning happiness, beauty, and perfection predates social media use, the difference is with social media we can look back at the performance and not seem bothered enough to change it.

For me, the question is not about whether we can stop performing, but when.

It's scary.

I do not enter this dialogue about social media without recognizing the serious harm social media inflicts on people's physical and mental well-being. Social media users spend hours each day scrolling through content that changes regularly and influences them on things like what to buy, eat and wear. I know we are all impacted by seeing only certain parts of each other and the negative space of what is left out from those conversations.

When I started using TikTok, the algorithm worked its way through figuring out my likes and dislikes based on what videos I interacted with. One content creator, Lydia Keating, caught my attention because of her running videos. I am a runner myself and may have gotten away from my cross-country days in high school, but seeing Lydia put time and effort into running inspired me. Lydia makes it clear she primarily runs to maintain her mental health. I related to her experiences, and because of this, I followed her and continued to enjoy the videos she shares.

As I continued to engage with Lydia's content, I was excited to learn she is also a writer, like me. On her TikTok page she began talking about getting a master's degree in creative writing. I remember watching Lydia unpack her belongings in her new room at school as she cleaned all the corners of her bedroom and situated herself. She talked about going for a run that day so she could cope with so much change and it reminded me of several times during and after college, when I did exactly that.

Lydia's content feels so genuine that I barely think of her as an influencer. But each time I run and put HOKAs on my feet, I remember I bought them because she swore by these sneakers for distance runners, and I felt I needed to have them myself. While I saw Lydia regularly post ads for sneakers and workout gear, I still didn't consider her an influencer because of how genuine her presence is. It feels silly to admit that's just one trick among many that make for successful marketing: convincing the viewer these moments of consuming content are much more candid and unplanned than they really are. Daily reminders that social media isn't real life can still feel tossed to the wayside when you don't question what you consume.

Not seeing Lydia as an influencer in the traditional sense, I was intrigued to see she wrote an article titled, "I am an influencer, and I think social media is toxic" for Slate. She began the article by explaining her role as a content creator, being paid for each post she shares, and the rules and guidelines she follows to make sure it's up to par for the company she works for.

Then she discussed a close family friend of hers who recently died by suicide. She talked about looking through [the family member's] Instagram, seeing a perfectly curated feed of someone who appears to be happy, confident, and free. Lydia used this example to illustrate how harmful performances can be, both for the performer and those who consume the performance. She reflected on her own sense of performance, stating that, "those harmful feelings—of worthlessness, body dysmorphia, loneliness, etc.—don't seem to arise as much when I am consuming others' content and their personal portrayals of false perfection, as when I am trying to present the false perfection of myself."

This stood out to me, mainly because it seems the idea of comparing ourselves to others would lead to unhealthy feelings about ourselves: insecurity, comparison, jealousy. But what Lydia says makes a lot of sense, too, as she shows no matter who she compares to, her self-worth faces its biggest obstacles when she portrays a version of herself that isn't true.

In this conversation of performance, I am reminded of one of my greatest role models, Brené Brown, best known for her discussions about vulnerability and courage. Brené teaches there is no vulnerability without courage. It is difficult to share and be brave, and one must have courage to do so. It is not meant to be easy, but rather high risk, high reward.

On social media we are not asked to be courageous or vulnerable. In fact, we are invited to do the opposite on a regular basis: sharing photos and videos of ourselves when we want, and in which we like how we present ourselves. We learn to share our opinions, but usually only when we are firm in them and less when we ask for clarity or admit what we don't know. The image we share with others of who we are becomes lacking in vulnerability, wrapped in ego, and a false sense of security.

There is no rule that states everyone needs to be completely and entirely themselves online. In fact, I don't know this would be the best solution. We need presence with each other in community to feel truly connected. However, I do think by continuing to use social media at the same frequency but failing to evolve in our use and ability to connect, we do ourselves a disservice.

There are times in my life where I have felt complete joy and deep sorrow, and in those moments, performing felt like an afterthought. For example, watching my friend's dad share his speech at her wedding, I let tears stream down my face in appreciation of their relationship and I didn't immediately go to the bathroom to fix my makeup. The moment was special and I'm so glad I was there for it. I also remember attending the funeral of a friend of mine who died while I was in college. I knew him well in high school but not as closely by the time of his funeral. The look in his parents' eyes stuck with me and I knew they would appreciate any memories shared of what their son, Elijah, meant to others. I got up and spoke, shaky and imperfect, looking at them as I spoke, not trying to be anyone besides someone who loved their son and wanted to share that with them.

I am grateful for these moments, both good and bad, in which I didn't perform anything but the most genuine feeling I had at the time. As I've mentioned, social media often appears as the antithesis to this feeling. But sometimes I feel we can make a compromise and connect to those very human, hard-to-misunderstand moments we have—to connect to what makes us who we are in a real sense: the people we have loved and the memories we have with them.

My guess is many people struggle with social media because it has historically felt like a space for performance. We begin to see each other as performers and we interpret ourselves as such. *What will my audience enjoy? What will they respond to? How can I elicit the response I want so I can feel confident and good about myself?*

I think it is natural and human to think of our social media presences this way. Most of us have a desire to be liked and to be likable, even when it gets in the way of authentic expression. On a small scale, it might prevent someone from sharing a post while wearing an outfit that isn't necessarily deemed on trend. On a larger scale, it may perpetuate a constant stream of updates that have little to no relation to one's real life and inner world.

As consumers of each others' real lives, we might sit back and see big cheeky grins and seemingly perfect bodies only to realize, too late, the suffering behind a perfectly curated performance.

Do we stop performing when we log out from social media and spend time with people we know, or do we sometimes act as if our audience is still watching, even when we know they aren't? Do we give ourselves space to be less than perfect and live a life that's not aesthetically beautiful at all times? Do we make space for moments of grief, crying, and pain?

Putting a stop to acting out perfection isn't easy. Think of how often you hear this dialogue pattern:

"Hey, how are you?"

"Good, you?"

"I'm good!"

Not only does this conversation drive me nuts, but it accomplishes *nothing* other than carry out a social requirement and adherence to a conversational pattern we can't seem to shake. I think of my Grammy, who almost always answers the question honestly:

"Not great, sweetie, I'm tired today."

"Awful. Have you seen the news?"

"I'm wonderful. The weather here is gorgeous. Have you been outside today?"

That's how you break the pattern and I think we can do this on social media as well. Just like we must notice the impulse to respond we are "good" in polite conversation, we need to notice the impulse to project what isn't true.

On the path to show up as ourselves, we need to begin with an easier step: don't show up as who you're not.

CHAPTER 3

OVERSHARING, OVERSHAMING

"This might be an overshare, but…"

This is how most of my favorite conversations with friends begin. I can think back to multiple instances when I was among a group of people and someone went out on a limb to talk about a problem they had.

"This might be an overshare, but, I have this weird thing on my back…"

"This might be an overshare, but, I was reading this article about…"

I've been on both ends of the overshare and will say no matter what you're about to say, it's scary. But we all know the best thing to hear in response to the overshare is,

"I'm SO glad you said something."

"Me too! I thought I was the only one."

I think it's interesting we refer to these moments as overshares because they usually end up bringing us closer to whoever we're with, through laughter or shared experience. The term overshare implies "too much" and begs for us to do and say less. But who does that benefit?

Personally, I love an overshare. I think it's powerful when people are willing to risk judgment for the sake of connection. There are so many human behaviors that prove, time and time again, humans are hard wired for connection. We want to know of others' experiences and have them see us for ours. So, wouldn't this lead us to believe taking our sharing into new spaces, like social media, would be a net positive?

Wrong.

After completing some preliminary research on the Internet about oversharing on social media, I realize journalists, psychologists, and others view oversharing quite negatively. A 2013 article in *HuffPost*, "Oversharing: Why Do we Do It and How Do We Stop?" says:

> "Experts say that oversharing is fueled by our insecurities, the need to compensate for deficits, socially or professionally that we perceive in ourselves. We worry about what others think, try desperately to make ourselves look good, giving away far more information than we should. When it doesn't work, which of course it wouldn't, we share even more."

The article breaks down several instances of oversharing, like a teenager posting photos after a surgery or parents posting about their children every day without their consent. It also discusses security risks (e.g., stalking, identity theft), which are valid. The end of the article provides suggestions on how to stop oversharing. It makes me laugh to think of someone going to Google and desperately typing "how to stop oversharing on social media." I am further intrigued by this part of that same article:

> "Imagine the ripple effect of the piece of information you are about to share. Imagine your mother, children, partner/spouse, boss, and any other relevant person knowing what you are about to divulge. Imagine meeting new people who possess the piece of information you are about to disclose."

I see there is some relevance to this argument, and everyone, on some level, should consider how sharing their daily lives and stories will impact people. It's hard to find any proof of a time when "oversharing," as we see it now, has benefited others. However, I can think of a few.

Remember #MeToo? Talk about a ripple effect.

The #MeToo movement started in 2006 when Tarana Burke created a Myspace page to increase visibility for youth survivors of sexual assault. As a survivor herself, she reflected on what helped her process her own experience. "When I started putting the pieces together of what helped me, it was having other survivors empathize with me," she told the *Washington Post* in 2017.

The Myspace page grew beyond what Tarana Burke originally imagined, realizing both youths and adults needed a space to share about their experiences with sexual assault. Many people, however, became familiar with the #MeToo movement in 2017 when Alyssa Milano reintroduced it as a response to the allegations against Harvey Weinstein. "If you've been sexually harassed or assaulted write 'me too' as a reply to this tweet," she wrote on her Twitter account.

I remember scrolling through Facebook and seeing friends post "MeToo," some of whom had disclosed their sexual assault to me previously and others who hadn't. For me, the moment was simultaneously heavy and empowering. I was in college at the time and although I attended a small school, I knew that each day I walked among people whose lives I would never know about firsthand. Social media changed that.

I know that the #MeToo movement had an impact on me. At its beginning, it made me realize more of my friends were survivors of sexual assault than not. And, more of them would go on to uncover sexual trauma in their past in later years. Today, #MeToo has over three million posts on Instagram alone. I reflect on Tarana Burke's bravery in her original Myspace post and again when Alyssa Milano posted on Twitter. I know these posts weren't shared without thought and consideration for their impact. In fact, they were shared so they *could* have an impact, and they did.

It's hard to quantify the difference between sharing and oversharing. Something that stands out to me is the concept of norms. In a lot of cases there isn't necessarily a right or wrong, just a norm. Imagine if one survivor of sexual assault, on their own, posted a long narrative about their assault without the solidarity of the #MeToo movement. Would it have done anything? The context here matters, and it was that the hashtag and visibility behind the movement that normalized the stories and invited them to the forefront.

Tarana knew the empathy of her community had helped her and she wanted to continue that in an online space. But it was also a reminder, on a large scale, of a systemic evil in our society that allows for the continued sexual violence we know exists.

At the end of the day, I wonder if we turn our noses up at oversharing because it feels like too much information, or if we are culturally uncomfortable with confronting that which reminds us of our own shame. To acknowledge we live in a society where crimes of sex and power happen at all levels feels overwhelming. Many people don't want to acknowledge it.

Drawing a connection between shame and sexual violence makes sense to me. What's harder to understand is the connection between shame and grief or loss. If we consider the fact that a vast majority of people experiencing grief and loss face situations largely out of their control, what reason would there be to feel ashamed about that? Do people feel ashamed about it?

Michael Cruz Kayne started his podcast, *A Good Cry*, on September 6, 2021. Twelve years prior to starting the podcast, Michael and his wife, Carrie, endured a complicated pregnancy with twins who had twin-to-twin transfusion syndrome, meaning the nutrients going to each twin were being dispersed unevenly. Though Truman survived, Fisher did not. In *A Good Cry*, Kayne cited his grief story as the reason why he wants to talk to others about grief.

In his mission to speak with "comedians and other notable types," he talks to writer and actress Megan Neuringer about the death of her twin sister and both of her parents. At age nine, Megan and her sister, Sybil, were walking home from school when Sybil was hit by a car. After a few days in a coma, she died. Later in life, Megan's parents both died from cancer.

Megan talked about the attention she has received in response to Sybil's and her parents' deaths on the podcast: "As somebody who's had major losses [...] for so long I didn't want to be seen as a victim of anything [...] it felt shameful and weird. I'm a weirdo for having so much loss!"

I understand the idea she communicates as much as someone who isn't in her shoes could. Loss is isolating and it brings up feelings of shame. What doesn't make sense to me, though, is *why*. Death is the one thing we can guarantee we will see in our lifetimes. Everyone will lose someone, yet when it happens, it can feel so personal and isolating, as if we are alone in that loss.

Megan went on to talk about how, when meeting new people, she chose whether or not to share about the death of her sister and her parents. Questions like "do you have siblings?" or "what do your parents do?" can stir up vastly different responses among people based on their experiences.

Megan struggled with whether to tell the truth immediately or skirt around the question. "You end up oversharing just by answering a polite question," she said.

I get this. It can feel awful when you share something as a response to an innocent question and someone looks at you with a blank stare or doesn't know what to say next. I think it can feel inherently shameful to share something close to our hearts and feel misunderstood. While I can talk myself blue in the face saying that shame shouldn't exist within us just for that reason, I know it's a common thing and people deal with it all the time.

For a lot of reasons, I'm not willing to accept this as the truth and move on. When grief and loss are so prevalent, I know I can't remove those feelings, but I hope to uncover solutions that remove the shame of having those feelings in the first place. As a former student in women's and gender studies, I have come to root much of my thought process in how intersectional feminism and theory inform today's norms. When it comes to feeling shame over grief and loss, is there something we can learn from feminism?

Thinking about this concept for a while, a term that kept coming back to me over and over again was "consciousness raising." The concept of consciousness raising is, quite literally, exactly what it says: to raise consciousness or awareness about something. It seems simple, but its impact is important.

In the 1970s, two nurses in the field of psychology, Bonnie Moore Randolph and Clydene Ross-Valliere, wanted to "mend rifts between the nursing profession and the women's movement" (Blakemore 2021). They started consciousness raising groups where women could share personal narratives about their experiences as women to connect and understand each other's experiences more.

Because personal narrative was at the root of all the conversations, it was much easier to connect and problem-solve together. "By the late 1970s, consciousness raising had helped thousands of women identify the causes of emotions they had once experienced as personal failings instead of the effects of a deeply patriarchal system" (Blakemore 2021).

This is powerful to me. I imagine during this time many women felt any shortcomings in their personal lives or conflicts in their careers were merely issues within them rather than issues reflective of society at large. Living this way makes it difficult to connect with others on these so-called shortcomings. Instead, women tend to internalize false messaging about their self-worth and value.

So, what does this have to do with grief and loss?

According to a 2020 AARP study on caregivers, more than one in five Americans are caretakers for adults or children with special needs. A 2022 article from The Recovery Village also cites about 2.5 million people in the US die each year, leaving an average of 5 grieving people behind. In addition, The Recovery Village estimates 1.5 million children (5 percent of children in the United States) have lost one or both parents by age fifteen. According to World Health Organization (WHO), suicide, the second leading cause of death in the US, takes the lives of approximately 800,000 people each year.

Beyond numbers and statistics, these are reminders we are likely interacting with people on a daily basis who have experienced major loss or are going through a process of grief we might not understand. These parts of our world are prevalent, but they are easy to ignore when we live in a culture that celebrates perfection and individualism and struggles to encourage community and sharing.

So why, then, are there over thirty-five million Instagram posts listed under #Joy and 160 million under #Happiness, but only two million posts under #Grief, two million under #Loss, and five million under #Death? Some may say it's just a level of boundaries—that we are only meant to share certain information online to begin with.

I would argue there is more to it than that. I think the lack of visibility of people's individual hardships is due to a culture of shame. To express grief over a loved one's death could be interpreted by others as an inability to move on. To share about an ongoing caretaking process could lead people to judge one's illness in a culture that idolizes physical well-being and upward mobility. To talk about a painful divorce could lead people to judge the separated couple as if they are failures themselves.

What would happen if we normalized these things? We might realize that instead of forcing ourselves to move on from a loss, we should confront the culture that pressures us to do so in the first place. Instead of vilifying people for mental or physical illness, we might reflect on the systems preventing or stopping these people from receiving proper support. Instead of seeing relationships as failures, we might consider that much of what we learn about love and relationships is lacking.

I mentioned my love for overshares, ones that tend to be funny or silly and easily shared over brunch with close friends. But, I also love the overshares that take bravery and vulnerability. I think we can learn from them and I hope we take the opportunity to do so. It isn't necessarily normal right now to post a photo of yourself after losing a pregnancy, signing divorce papers, or experiencing the death of someone you love, but some people are doing it anyways.

Even if I initially wonder why someone would share a moment like that, I then consider what about their vulnerability makes me uncomfortable and if I could get past that. I also consider what I can learn from their experience as they've chosen to make it public. A silly overshare between friends, to me, is an invitation to be more open about my daily experiences, while a more serious sharing about grief and loss is a moment to connect with myself and others in a powerful way that feels larger than me.

So, the next time you think something you're about to say is an "overshare," consider this: will it set you free? Could it set us all free?

CHAPTER 4

"HANDLING IT": INDIVIDUALISM AS THE ANTITHESIS TO COMMUNITY

According to Health Resources and Services Administration, seventeen people die each day waiting for an organ transplant. That's over six thousand people each year who die in the waiting period, let alone those who die posttransplant. Luckily, I did not know these statistics before my dad received his new liver.

While waiting for a transplant, my sister, Ashlyn, decided we needed a second opinion. She wanted to look at the services offered at University of Pittsburgh Medical Center (UPMC) to see if their transplant team was more equipped to handle our dad's needs than the treatment he was receiving locally. Up until that point, the only possibility available to him was to eventually be listed for transplant and wait for a cadaver liver, which meant he could be waiting indefinitely until someone who was an organ donor with a viable liver passed away.

When we started working with UPMC, we learned they offered the option of receiving the transplant via a living donor. Since the liver regenerates, this means a healthy person can donate a portion of their liver to someone in need and still be able to live a normal, healthy life afterward. While this seems simple, we also learned the recovery process can be very involved for the donor, at the same time bringing health and a new life force for the recipient.

Around June 2021 my sister and I had to determine roles for ourselves, namely Caregiver and Champion. The Caregiver was the primary person who would be able to take care of the patient in their recovery, while the Champion was someone who would take on the responsibility of finding a living donor for the patient. While we shared these roles with each other and didn't necessarily divide them in the way they were explained, we gave the hospital the appropriate contact information for her, Caregiver, and me, Champion. I received a thick binder about my role as the Champion and couldn't help but think this was the most absurd task a person could be faced with.

I read the pamphlets and watched videos of people talking about how they managed to successfully find a willing donor through social media or other networks they had. At this point, my dad was receiving chemoembolization treatments for his liver cancer and his energy was dwindling, as was his hope of ever receiving a transplant. He talked to us regularly about how he was ready to share his story more widely and be able to find a living donor. This was new for us. Up until that point, we tended to handle these matters as a family and keep to ourselves.

The idea of opening up to a wider audience about our family's needs at the time felt overwhelming to me. Up until that point, I'd only posted minimally to close friend groups on my Instagram about my dad not doing well. Generally, I didn't share specifics and wanted to be respectful of his process and Ashlyn as well, who tends to be more private about her life on social media. But on top of this, as someone who feels awkward asking for monetary donations at my nonprofit job, the idea of asking someone to donate an organ and suffer through the recovery process felt like a favor none of us would ever be able to repay. I struggled with knowing where to start and how to balance my own fear of judgment with the fact that the situation was becoming more and more severe. It was hard to ignore the secret ticking clock that loomed over us each day.

Reflecting on how I felt about opening up and making such a large ask made me realize part of the shame I carried reflected a wider cultural expectation to not rely on others. I've tried to dissect why, exactly, I felt so uncomfortable with sharing our story more widely. I've wondered what messaging I received in my personal life and from society at large that made me feel relying on my community during struggle was wrong. Why did I feel such a strong inclination to solve this issue without asking for the support of my community?

This moment of uncertainty and fear reminded me of a class I took in college called "Health, Illness, and Narrative". It was outside of my major but the curriculum sounded interesting, so I enrolled. The point of the class was to analyze how a culture of individualism, like we have in the United States, exists at the opposite end of the needs of those who are ill. We talked about physical and mental illnesses and read some of the most impactful texts I remember from my college career.

We started the course reading a book called *Ragged Dick* by Horatio Alger, published in 1867. Alger became so famous for his style of books that the term "Horatio Alger story" became indicative of any story about someone who gets themselves out of poverty with hard work and honesty. In *Ragged Dick*, a fourteen-year-old homeless boy, Dick, spends his days shining shoes and offering kindness to those around him when he can. He has several interactions with wealthier people in the community who pride themselves on their own rags-to-riches stories and convince Dick it's a realistic path in life. When Dick goes on a ferry to Brooklyn, he sees a small boy drowning in the water and saves him. He later learns he saved the son of James Rockwell, a famous industrialist and financier. James gives Dick a job, which absolves him of his financial struggle and changes the trajectory of his life entirely.

In class, we talked about how absurd this narrative was, noting how in many instances people have worked incredibly hard and been kind to those around them, only to realize it's not enough to achieve financial stability in our complicated socioeconomic system. We also spent a lot of time talking about how the idea of individualism and "pulling yourself up by your bootstraps" isn't applicable to everyone. As we moved into reading memoirs assigned for the semester, it felt like we could, together, uncover some of the harsh truths about how mental and physical illness stand at a stark contrast to the idea that being a dedicated and independent person can single-handedly get you everywhere you need to be.

My favorite book of the semester was *The Cancer Journals* by Audre Lorde, who describes herself as a "Black, lesbian, mother, warrior, poet." I loved *The Cancer Journals*, in part because I was already familiar with Lorde's work, but only within the context of her activism as an intersectional feminist. Until this course I hadn't realized Lorde also had breast cancer at one point and had a mastectomy. I remember reading the essays and diary entries that came to make up *The Cancer Journals* and feeling strangely connected to Lorde because of her purposeful and precise writing. I felt in awe of her ability to write through the challenges she faced so that they might encourage others to see the world differently.

Lorde not only had to undergo a procedure to remove part of her body, but she was also judged for this decision as it was referred to by the staff at her doctor's office as "bad for morale." Identifying as a Black lesbian as well, she sat at the margins of society and risked further separation from her communities by having cancer and choosing to make that experience visible rather than hide it. In *The Cancer Journals*, she talks about the difficulty of establishing her identity up until a certain point in life and then not knowing where the blueprints were for others like her who experienced illness.

The meaning of this story stuck with me. I don't think I understood the gravity Audre Lorde's words would have on me and I know I will never fully understand many parts of her story. But her cries for community, being seen, and not having to disappear because of her illness indicate a major flaw in our society I know still exists. One of Audre Lorde's largest impacts, in my view, was her commitment to transforming silence into language and action. She knew to write and communicate her life experiences would not only remove a veil of silence around herself, but would also mobilize others to see things can change.

Although *The Cancer Journals* was written in the 1980s, I fear we still uphold many of these pressures as a society to handle every challenge on an individual basis, ignoring the value of community. Thinking back to how many people die each day waiting for an organ transplant leads me to wonder if those people had the support they needed or knew where to go for solidarity.

I didn't have to undergo any surgery or sacrifice my physical appearance to help my dad, but I did learn to swallow my pride so we could get what we needed. I realized in this process that to ask for help from my community would make me feel exposed and vulnerable but could have long-lasting benefits.

I started by making a private Facebook page for people who were close to our family and regularly involved with updates on our dad's health. I tried to generate content the way I believed a social media manager would, posting statistics, stories, and updates. It felt strange and not representative of my voice as his daughter. But to connect with those emotions at the time would have made the process almost impossible, I think.

Eventually, my sister suggested we also have a public page for his story to be more widely shared and, hopefully, help us find a donor. I remember the day I made the public page "Ron's Liver Transplant." I shared a lengthy first post about what we were asking for and how to help. I invited hundreds of people to like the page and sat, watching, while likes came in through notifications.

While I had written blog posts before about my personal life, something about this felt even more vulnerable to me because I needed something from other people. It was also one of the first times in my life I used social media in a new functional way, out of necessity rather than a way to pass time or casually socialize.

Although a few people showed interest, we were never able to find a living donor through this method. By September 2021, my dad learned his eligibility for a transplant had increased due to a somewhat intricate number system they apply to all transplant patients. What this meant was we could get a call any day to come in for an unscheduled transplant, but if he were to find a living donor himself the process could be expedited. By the end of that week, on October 1st, my dad got the call to come in for surgery because they had a viable liver for him.

We never learned much about the donor other than he was a healthy man in his fifties who died unexpectedly. I remember feeling overwhelmed by many parts of the transplant process. One of them was the realization my dad was given a chance at a better, healthier life while someone's had unexpectedly ended. It's something I can't possibly take for granted.

Once my dad underwent his transplant, with some complications, Ashlyn and I had more time to update our channels of communication. I posted in the Ron's Liver Transplant group to inform everyone he was two weeks posttransplant and doing well. I thanked them for following along with the journey and asked for prayers and support as we moved through a new phase of the process.

When I reflect on this experience now, I see I was being challenged to accept that not all things can be solved alone, although it would be so satisfying if that were the truth. The reality is, although we weren't able to find a liver donor through the shared group, what we did find was a sense of community we might not have found. Knowing there was a community of people, who were up to speed and there for us made a huge difference.

I also realize I most likely would not have created this sense of community had I not felt it was the only option. While I'm grateful to have had a support network, I am saddened to realize this is likely not the common experience of most people. If there were no solutions for my dad's health, we would have suffered in silence. If there was no need for others' help, we would have continued living as we were. This is not normal—in fact, it's harmful. A 2015 article published by *Time* magazine suggests loneliness could potentially be the next public health crisis. "More Americans are living alone than ever before, and technology like texting and social media has made it easier to avoid forming substantive relationships in the flesh and blood."

With increased physical isolation and use of technology, it makes sense this combination would weaken the relationships we have with one another. It makes me wonder, though: if we used these digital platforms differently, could we mitigate some of the loneliness we feel? We are so accustomed to managing our daily problems it's as if the idea of community and support networks are secondary to everything else. We need to realize this was learned and to lean into community is a natural part of humanity.

In my case, I had to unlearn what I thought the unspoken rules were when it came to using social media. Instead of using it as a space for life updates or validation, I needed it to perform a function. By opening up and asking for what I needed, I felt closer to people and I would guess they felt the same. It broke down a barrier that is easy to uphold online when you can take time to think about how you want to present yourself and your life.

We experience some of the most valuable moments of our lives within our communities, such as weddings, funerals, and ceremonies. But these moments of struggle that punctuate those larger experiences are expected to be dealt with alone. We are taught we are braver and stronger to deal with things on our own and to manage the outcomes by ourselves.

I know this is a symptom of a culture that celebrates rising to the top through one's own means and not asking anyone for help along the way. A lot of us still think this way and many of us are only forced to reconsider that view when we need our community desperately, some people sooner than others.

I hope we can understand, before moments of desperation, how to build community and share our struggles so people around us can know us better and share life in a richer way.

David Kessler, a fundamental contributor to the literature on grief, notes in his book *Finding Meaning* a phenomenon in a northern Australian community after they experience a death. When someone in that community loses a family member, everyone in the surrounding area, overnight, brings a piece of furniture out on their front yard. This way, in the morning, the person who experienced the loss can see everything has changed. They know their community sees this too.

I contrast this with countless narratives I've heard from people the day after a major loss or during an ongoing grief process. The thought that cars would still pass by on the street, that people would still be going about their normal lives, feels wrong when you're in the midst of something so earth shattering.

I know not all of us will put furniture on our front lawns for each other in the near future unless a major cultural shift happens, but I do wonder what would happen if we released ourselves from the pressure of "handling it" alone.

CHAPTER 5

ALGORITHMS AND USER EXPERIENCES

"What's your deepest fear?"

If I was gay.

The thought was so loud I could have sworn someone heard me. I was at a sleepover with some other girls in my fifth-grade class. We sat in a circle after trying on all the clothes my friend Erika had in her closet. Following the traditional pattern of a young girls' slumber party, once we'd laughed enough and tried on enough clothes, the mood settled a bit. We were in the heart-to-heart portion of the slumber party.

Did I say it out loud? I must have. When it was my turn, I made up an answer, perhaps the dark or spiders. I still remember how strange it felt to think this thought and connect to the fear I had as a young person in a relatively conservative area. I really felt, at the time, being gay was one of the worst things I could be.

I don't remember knowing anyone who personally identified as LGBTQ+ at that age, but I do remember the whispers and speculations about people who might be. By high school I think there were a few people who were "out."

I came out as queer in college. I met several people in class and in my friend groups who were comfortable with their identities in more ways than one, and it was liberating for me to be around them. Although, it still took a few years of my own introspection to identify this way, surrounding yourself with people who are proud of who they are can be an invitation to do the same, but it can also feel painful in its own ways. It begs you to consider why you have not allowed yourself that same freedom.

After being out for a little while to my smaller community, I posted a photo of myself on Instagram on National Coming Out day during my junior year of college. The lengthy caption addressed my personal opinion that nobody should feel pressure to come out at all. I remember reading comments from people who celebrated what I shared, and admittedly, some of them made me feel strange. The people from my hometown who had never once spoken up for the LGBTQ+ community calling me a "badass" reminded me of the performative nature of social media. Still, though, I try to assume they intended to validate me in my moment of vulnerability.

I have since posted other times on National Coming Out day and been relatively open about how I identify, but haven't always felt like Instagram was my favorite place to share that information. The people I follow and those who follow me back are relatively static on that platform, meaning there are still people I know from high school I haven't spoken to in years who see the life updates I share. With this in mind, sharing on Instagram can feel, at times, like having a private conversation with a friend, only to realize someone still lingers in the room you had not noticed at first.

Sometime around March 2021 I finally downloaded TikTok, something I had previously rolled my eyes at because I thought it was an app for teenagers. Enough friends my age and older had started using TikTok after a surge in its popularity around the start of the COVID-19 pandemic and I was curious to learn more.

TikTok is a video-sharing platform with clips ranging from a couple seconds to a couple minutes, and it can be incredibly addicting. After downloading it, I was quickly hooked, but I also realized the platform exposed me to information that wasn't coming at me in the same way on other platforms. That is to say, the algorithm used my in-app activity to accurately learn what type of TikTok content I like and quickly brought me to those videos. What this means is, when you begin using TikTok, the app exposes you to a wide variety of content. Based on what you interact with—by liking the video or commenting, for example—your personal feed is created.

The "coming out" phenomenon of TikTok is one example of this process in action. Googling "TikTok thinks I'm gay" will bring up several results of people whose TikTok usage over time brought them to more and more LGBTQ+ content. Even if they joined TikTok and did not identify with this community, the content they interacted with steered them there. For some, this was simply a comical realization that changed nothing about their identity other than help them realize they are probably allies of the community and share many of our interests and values. For others, this was a pivotal moment in realizing they might have some more self-exploration to do.

I am fascinated by the accuracy of a platform that can observe one's likes and dislikes and be able to have this effect. While mostly comical in this example, what can we learn from it? It makes me wonder if certain social media platforms are better than others at bringing us closer to the communities we hope to connect with.

I think it is valuable to consider the different user experiences of each social media platform and figure out which one works well for your style and what you are looking for. The difficult thing about social media, I think, is we often turn to it to pass the time, which means we are not necessarily actively using the platforms. For example, I remember first signing up for Instagram and searching for certain people I wanted to follow and engage with more. Now, I rarely seek that out, but will from time to time follow a new person if I meet someone new in real life or connect that way.

Since downloading TikTok, I have developed a stronger interest in understanding why people use certain social media platforms and what they gain from them. After using the same platforms for years, namely Instagram, Twitter and Facebook, there was a newness to the TikTok experience that made me more analytical of how I have engaged with social media in the past and present. With the expansion of platforms, it's interesting to see what needs or desires each platform fulfills for people.

I've enjoyed asking other people who use social media what their favorite platform is and why. Common responses are Reddit, TikTok, Twitter, and Instagram. One person might enjoy the nuance you can find in a Reddit thread, whereas the next might enjoy the visual and luxurious depictions of life you can find on Instagram, and another person might enjoy the anonymity of TikTok. A 2020 study published by Counseling Today, that explores the topic of social media and therapy, suggests therapists ask their clients what their social media does for them too.

> *"If a client really loves TikTok, have them walk you through it: What do they like about it? What makes a good video [post]? What do they engage with the most? This helps open them up and tells you a lot about why and how they engage [...] It gives you a better idea about their motivation, their mindset, and their personality based on the type of platform and how they engage [with it]."*

There are a lot of reasons why I think people choose certain platforms over others and certain people, like myself, dabble in several platforms. When I joined TikTok, I immediately had a full feed of anonymous users whose videos I could choose to engage with or swipe past. The For You Page is basically the landing page of the app and the main place where people spend their time while using the app. You can scroll for hours watching videos and not see anyone you know.

Comparatively, when I log into Twitter, I am mostly met with a feed full of thoughts and ideas from people I chose to follow. Those people may or may not follow me back and engage with my ideas. In more recent updates to Twitter's algorithm, the addition of a "based on tweets you like" feature has opened up my feed to tweets from those I may not follow, but whose content seems relatable to me based on what I've engaged with up until that point.

The Instagram algorithm has changed quite a bit over time as well. Part of this is due to the extreme success of TikTok's incredibly accurate algorithm. Instagram's changes include a chronological feed, meaning you see posts from people you follow in the order they were shared. It also includes a favorites feed, which is a second feed of up to fifty accounts you also enjoy. On Instagram you can follow people and hashtags you find interesting and also tap your explore page to find content beyond what you follow that you might also like.

When I reflect on my fifth-grade self who knew something about herself but was not ready to admit it, I think about what was at my fingertips that could have helped. I don't remember many, if any, LGBTQ+ influences in the literature I read in school and never found it in the books I read by myself. I didn't know anyone around me who shared my thoughts, and because of that, I felt ashamed.

I think about how differently I feel about myself as a queer person now. Part of that change in mindset is due to the community I found in college. I also accredit some of this confidence to the access I have to social media. Even after being out for a few years, the expansive nature of social media that allows me to see queer and trans people across the globe, living and dressing how they want and expressing their thoughts, is a unique experience my younger self would be so excited to know I have now. My younger self waited for permission to know it was okay to be authentically her, and my current self is regularly reminded it is more than okay.

In this way, I think we can shift our understanding of social media and how content comes to us through algorithms. Rather than seeing it as invasive, we could consider these algorithms help expedite the process of finding our people and creating connections with ideas and experiences that resonate with us. Social justice dialogue regularly affirms the importance of representation of diverse identities within media like film and television shows; it is a very human thing to want to see our experiences reflected in what we consume.

So how does that translate to grief?

Just like understanding one's sexuality, grief and loss are very personal and often invisible experiences too. One of my favorite artists and writers, Mari Andrew, published an article titled "Grief Baby" in February 2021, marking the seven years since her father's death. She personified her grief into a seven-year-old child.

"Seven: a second grader, a blossoming individual, someone who can read to themselves, someone who still likes to be tucked in at night." Mari remembers the time immediately after her father's death, when her grief was a newborn, and she was sleep deprived and "ill equipped to understand its wants and needs." I love the way she chooses to personify and characterize her grief.

Any parent will say parenting never really ends, but just changes over time. We often don't have the understanding, though, to see grieving never ends either, but also changes over time. While a parent might hold photos of their children in their wallet or walk hand in hand with their seven year old, Mari carries her invisible-grief baby with her everywhere in life, though people may never see it.

In a culture that places pressure on grieving people to move on, it makes sense those who process grief might stop sharing about it with the people closest to them after some time. One day, my friend sent me a TikTok video of a twenty-seven-year-old woman named Carson who lost both of her parents in the same year. Carson's profile is full of videos explaining what happened to her parents and how she processes her grief journey through the days that have followed.

In the video my friend shared, Carson addresses the fact she shares personal information about her grief for strangers on the Internet, knowing it might seem strange to some. "When you are grieving, you feel like a burden on your friends and family. You feel like every time you talk about it, you are dragging them down into the pits of your depression with you," she says.

Carson concludes the video by saying she chooses to share her grief with strangers because it's where she has been able to connect with others and find more people who understand her situation. The caption of her video includes two hashtags: #grief and #griefjourney. On TikTok, this means anyone who already engages with grief content is more likely to find this video as well.

I think, more than anything, we want to feel connected to others because it helps us feel connected to ourselves. It feels terrible to be misunderstood or misinterpreted. On the other hand, the healing that can come from feeling seen and validated is transformative. It makes sense that if people feel less comfortable expressing their grief in their immediate circles, they would resort to other places like social media, even if just to share their story with complete strangers looking to connect and relate.

I don't have an invisble-grief baby like Mari Andrews does, but at a certain point in my journey with my dad's health, I felt as if I was gestating one of my own. It took a while to know what was going on, but as things progressed with his diagnosis, I stopped understanding my own behavior and felt less and less connected to myself. I didn't want to talk about the future anymore because it scared me. I questioned everything I said or did to my friends and colleagues because I lost trust in myself.

I learned in therapy this is called anticipatory grief, when one anticipates the loss of someone close to them. Once I knew this, I was more comfortable identifying with having an experience of grief. Previously I thought you had to experience a death to claim that, but as I validated this unique experience, I started engaging more with content online about grief as well. Just like learning about my sexuality, understanding my grief was another personal process that took time.

This time, I had a place to turn, and I knew how to find what I needed. The more I engaged with, the more I was given.

I follow grief accounts on all social media platforms and often send posts that resonate with me to my sister. It has helped us connect and put words to the things we think and feel. There is power in allowing ourselves to identify with grief so we can learn more about it and understand how to process it individually and together.

Seeing grief content on my social media feeds also punctuates the highlight reel content I sometimes experience in those spaces. I am reminded other people carry grief with them too and some people spend the bulk of their days helping others process how to hold that weight. As I get older, my fears about life and the future change. Something I can lean on is knowing I have resources and I can find connections, and that helps.

People want to feel connected.

CHAPTER 6

FINDING COMMUNITY

"Rarely, if ever, are any of us healed in isolation. Healing is an act of communion"

-BELL HOOKS, *ALL ABOUT LOVE*

Prior to my dad's illness, I probably associated the word "caregiver" with women much older than me, because that's what I'd seen the most. Growing up, I knew a few older women who cared for their elderly mom or dad. But as a twenty-five year old, I wasn't sure where other people like myself or my sister were. When I reflect on this now, I consider the fact I had a desire for community but had absolutely no idea how to find it or if it existed.

Just weeks before my dad received his liver transplant, my sister invited me to join a closed Facebook group for caregivers of liver transplant patients. She told me she found the group by doing some research, in hopes of connecting with people who could tell us more about what to expect from the process. Although we were given thick binders that included information on what takes place during a liver transplant, how to find a donor, and other preparatory materials, we knew very little of what would happen when he actually got the call.

What were the risks? What would recovery look like? What does life look like posttransplant? I know I hadn't even begun to think of some of these factors, but my sister needed a clearer picture and I'm so grateful she found a community for us.

When joining the caregivers' group, I was intrigued to realize there were a few ground rules before I could join. First, the community was strictly meant for caregivers of transplant patients and not for patients themselves, and no soliciting or advertising was allowed.

> *"This group is a private, secure space for caregivers only of liver transplant patients to come together for questions, discussion, support, comfort, and strength through our difficult journey. Support from other caregivers during this life changing transplant process is vital to our personal well-being."*

This was the message on the right-hand side when I looked at the page, under a caption that said, "READ BEFORE REQUESTING TO JOIN. ALL REQUESTS ARE SCREENED."

I entered the community space not knowing what to expect but quickly realized the posts were frequent and varied in subject matter. Some caregivers excitedly posted when their loved one was ready for transplant and others asked for advice postop for major weight loss, medication rejection, and other complications that may arise.

Soon, I realized something as niche as a liver transplant was full of community. In the caregiver group, we were encouraged to introduce ourselves upon joining. I was shy to introduce myself but ended up posting something in the group about two weeks after my dad received his liver transplant and while we were still in the hospital with him during his recovery. I tagged my sister in the post and let everyone know we were his caregivers and that he was doing well postop and likely to be discharged soon.

Looking back on the welcome messages under my post, I am reminded of how comforted I felt knowing others were with us.

"Welcome to posttransplant!" said one woman, followed by several heart emojis.

"I'm glad to hear your dad received his gift and is doing well!" said another.

"No question is to be not asked, rest your minds." This one makes me cry, even now.

Feeling welcomed in that space helped me acknowledge I had arrived somewhere. So much of the process felt like trying to avoid ending up at the worst places; I hadn't considered I could arrive somewhere else. It was a place where everyone knew that a higher MELD score (model for end-stage liver disease) meant we were one step closer to transplant. It was a place where people knew the names of all the antirejection medications someone might be taking and suggestions for when they cause certain symptoms.

We had wonderful medical professionals throughout the experience, but the caregivers' group, as an extension of the experience at large, provided the sense of community and solidarity I didn't even realize I needed.

Now, whenever I log onto Facebook, my timeline is peppered with posts from the caregiver group I often stop to read. I love to see the posts where people receive the call we did and start the next phase of the journey: transplant. I also know it is a difficult journey and feel sad alongside other caregivers when they run into complications pre or postop. Reading the messages of support reminds me how important it is to turn to others.

I recognize now the use of the term "vital" in the welcome message is not at all an exaggeration, although I may have read it that way to begin with. We needed this support system and can see how much it helped us. What would happen if we hadn't had this network?

When I'm 64 is a podcast hosted by Ken Stern that emerged as a response to the COVID-19 pandemic. The podcast covers various aspects of caregiving in the United States, from Seth Rogen and Lauren Miller Rogen's work to fund Alzheimer's research, to the challenges of caregiving for military veterans.

In an episode from September 2020, the podcast covered the specific challenges of millennial caregivers. On behalf of

AARP, Jean Accius shared some insights from research that uncovered the unique experiences and challenges within this age group. "Society doesn't think of millennials as caregivers," he shared, explaining that while caregiving is tough for all age groups, it is particularly tough for millennials. The general dismissal of young people as caregivers is one of the many challenges.

During the episode, a young caregiver, Libby Brittain, talked about taking care of her mother during her early-onset Alzheimer's. Libby admitted she did not immediately label herself as a caregiver and only began thinking of herself as one a couple years into the process of caregiving. Without more general cultural understanding of the experiences of young caregivers, it would make sense she did not immediately see herself as one.

"In many cases [millennial caregivers] felt isolated and many of their friends could not relate or understand what they were going through," Accius stated. He went on to talk about the professional and financial concerns for millennial caregivers, stating they are less likely to report to a supervisor they are in a caregiving role and, oftentimes, more likely to receive a warning at work due to performance issues when caregiving. Financially, millennial caregivers are at a higher risk for financial strain than other age groups and most likely to be unable to afford basic expenses on top of caregiving expenses.

Considering the professional and financial challenges of caregiving in combination with the feelings of isolation that it can bring, it seems like a particularly tough situation to find community. And, as I talked about in my own experience, I certainly was not sure how to cultivate that community for myself until I was invited into a space where it already existed.

Whether outwardly sharing an experience or searching for a smaller community to share in solidarity, I believe social media can be used as a powerful tool to connect through the experiences that are most difficult in life. I think the challenging part, though, is realizing community can exist in these spaces in the first place. We might not be conditioned to immediately seek out people who reflect our experiences even though it's helpful. We might not be comfortable sharing the experience as it happens. We might not know sharing about what we go through could help others.

Luckily, there are leaders in many spaces who do recognize this need for connection and community. They cultivate it by sharing their experiences with others. Through my work in oral history, I remembered a woman who came to record with a close friend of hers about their journeys as caretakers. Her name is Jacquelyn Revere, but on TikTok she is known as @MomofMyMom. She agreed to share more about the impetus behind starting her TikTok account when I told her I was hoping to learn more.

Jacquelyn cared for her mom, who had been dealing with Alzheimer's for about five years at the time of our conversation. When she stepped into her caregiving role, she looked for other caretakers in similar positions as her but came up empty. So, she created the community she wanted to see. Jacquelyn started posting TikToks of herself and her mother's journey. The first of her videos that went viral was of her mother lovingly pointing at a picture of a young Jacquelyn and referring to her as "mommy."

"Are you calling me mommy?" Jacquelyn clarifies in the video.

"That's my mommy," says her mom.

Watching her mother point at a picture of young Jacquelyn and refer to her as her own mother was a powerful moment for Jacquelyn and it illustrated a shift that happens within caretaking. As the primary caretaker for her mother, Jacquelyn performs a lot of duties one would also see a mother doing with a young child. She cooks meals, nurtures, and looks out for her mother. Although she isn't literally her mom's mom, this experience of caretaking and the shift in responsibility led Jacquelyn to use @MomofMyMom for her account name to share about the experience.

As she watched the views climb on her video, Jacquelyn was flooded with comments from people experiencing similar situations with their parents. Some of them even mentioned their moms refer to them as "mom" as well. Jacquelyn's followers grew exponentially after she posted that video, which to me speaks to the importance of her content as an open door for people who need it. She continues to share TikToks of her and her mom but has expanded her reach with speaking engagements and other public relations opportunities.

Before her mom's diagnosis, Jacquelyn worked in the television and film industry, and like many caretakers, has put some of her dreams on hold to be there for her mom. But sharing on social media about their journey helps her tie some of her personal dreams into the reality of daily life with her mom.

"The social media account that I have plays into what I believe my purpose here is. It plays into what I've studied and what I've always been very passionate about, but now I get to do it with my mom," she told me. "I don't know what could be better than taking something that I was very passionate about and taking the time that I have learned with my mom and finding those to then help other people."

I can see Jacquelyn helps people on a regular basis by responding to comments and sharing tips and information about her own journey. Some people who join the page will share with Jacquelyn their loved one was recently diagnosed and they are scared for what's to come. I imagine merely scrolling through Jacquelyn's videos is an inherent comfort to someone who wouldn't know what to expect or who to reach out to.

When I spoke to Jacquelyn in December 2021, she was in full-time caregiving mode for her mom. On March 9, 2022, Jacquelyn shared a TikTok letting everyone know her mother had passed. She shared very few details other than stating everyone was with her when it happened and "she's dancing in heaven now."

In the following weeks, Jacqueline continued to share about losing her mom and the specific parts of grief people may never consider until they experience it themselves. For example, she didn't want to throw certain food items away that were reminders of her mom. Jacquelyn shared videos from her mom's service and reflections of her own grief process as she continued to move through new moments in life that challenged her. She even made videos explaining what people can say to those in grief and what she hopes they won't say. In the comments, people thanked her, admitting they sometimes struggled to have the right words to say to others in grief.

For me, it is powerful to watch a community grieve with Jacquelyn. Many people shared that just by watching these TikToks over time, they felt so connected to Jacquelyn and her mom that the loss was incredibly visceral for them as well. Jacqueline's willingness to share offers her the ability to engage with others and accept words of encouragement and connection she might have missed out on during this loss.

In both mine and Jacquelyn's stories, social media was the catalyst that allowed us to connect with communities otherwise out of our reach. With a following of over six hundred thousand people, Jacquelyn brought people together in an experience of caretaking that rarely receives visibility on social media platforms. Her success on TikTok is an indicator of the need for this sort of visibility.

As life moves forward, we engage in social networks based on shared experiences, such as friendships formed from the shared experience of college, a job, or a workout group. But when someone goes through a loss or a life change like becoming a caretaker, this process is halted. Life becomes focused on the new situation at hand and a lot of times feels like survival more than anything else.

To me, community is a survival technique the individualist culture of American society often neglects. Instead of embracing community, people take on new challenges and believe they are meant to do it alone so as not to burden those around them. But what we can see in the power of Jacquelyn's vulnerability and commitment to sharing is she finds value and meaning in that process. By sharing her story, she connects with a massive network of people who care about her journey and want to learn more.

For myself, being part of the caregivers' group also allows me the opportunity to surrender some of my fears to a communal space. I remember this experience does not need to feel isolating and people are here to help.

Mine and Jacquelyn's stories also show there are different approaches to finding community on social media. I recognize not all people feel comfortable sharing their lives outwardly on social media, regardless of the content. This is where a private group with more specific boundaries and rules, like the caregivers Facebook group, comes in handy. This is a place where I felt safe to express my worries and offer advice to complete strangers, because they knew I had a shared experience I did not need to prove or explain. While we can see the names and profiles of those who post in the group, there is a sense of anonymity because we interact within the group on the shared experiences we have and nothing else.

Jacquelyn's approach to community is one I admire a lot; I think it takes more bravery than most people would consider.

Sharing videos about her mom's Alzheimer's goes directly against the "highlight reel" norm that dominates discussions about social media and it does not come without criticism. I have read through hateful and dismissive comments on her videos that show there are many people who have never walked in her shoes. I commend Jacquelyn for addressing these issues and for staying true to her content because of the way it benefits all the people who need it.

On social media we often only see what is already there. We are not trained to see the negative space—what is missing or what we wish to see. I certainly did not consider social media would be a space for me to connect with others in my shoes and I imagine others feel that way too.

My suggestion is that we shift our perspective on the spaces we engage in on social media. Become an active and engaged participant rather than simply accepting what comes our way. Whatever platform you use most often, reflect on the first five to ten posts you see when you log on. Do you relate to them? Do they bring you joy, comfort, or deeper understanding? Do they inspire you to know yourself better or connect with others? If you are in grief or experiencing a loss, consider this as well. Are you connected to others in grief and loss? Have you considered ways of finding that community?

I know some people struggle with the mere task of asking for help; it feels clunky and vulnerable. We are taught to shoulder life's hardships alone, assuming someday our independence will be rewarded. Not only does this push us to isolate ourselves; it also keeps people away who would otherwise love to help us. If we crave community in our biggest moments of joy, we need that same community when we are lost and hurting. Whether we create this community somewhere online or elsewhere in the world, it is important to know the capacity for it exists at all.

CHAPTER 7

WHEN WE HONOR THE LOVE, WE HONOR OURSELVES

―

Elizabeth Kübler-Ross was a Swiss-American psychiatrist best known for her book *On Death and Dying*. In her debut novel published in 1969, she coined what we now know as the five stages of grief: denial, anger, bargaining, depression, acceptance. This gave people language for their process and helped them in their grief. Today, *On Death and Dying* is considered a quintessential book for grieving people and one therapists often use to help grieving clients.

Kübler-Ross went on to coauthor *On Grief and Grieving* with grief expert and founder of Grief.com, David Kessler. No stranger to grief, Kessler lost his mom to severe health issues when he was only thirteen years old. His life's work became centered around providing resources for those who were also grieving. But as a father of two adult sons, his life changed when his son, David, died of an overdose at twenty-one years old.

"People thought there was an end to grief [...] you'd get to acceptance and be done [...] I needed to find meaning," he shared with Brené Brown on *Unlocking Us*, Brown's podcast. Not only did Kessler find meaning in his loss, but he also went on to publish *Finding Meaning: The Sixth Stage of Grief*. In it, he shared about how he worked through the grief of losing his son and shares stories of others who have found meaning in their loss as well.

"Ultimately, meaning comes through finding a way to sustain your love for the person after their death while you're moving forward with your life," he writes. I think this is a great point and one that might not be widely understood by people unfamiliar to grief.

I noticed Kessler does not suggest sustaining the *memory* of someone. He says love. Love, a verb, is sustained through intention and presence, and it continues to grow over time. To me, Kessler points out the way a relationship with someone who has passed can still develop. Instead of continuing to build the relationship on shared experiences and moments together, this shift might look like recognizing when you remember your loved one and when you share about them with others. It could look like a tattoo of remembrance, written songs, or journal entries.

What would this look like in a digital era?

In my early stages of research, I spent time speaking with people I knew who had shared about their grief on social media. I was also curious to speak to people I didn't know at all so I could see their social media narrative as any other newcomer would. I would have no context, no insider perspective. This brought me to Mike.

I found Mike through a LinkedIn post, a space where I had not previously established myself as someone who spoke about grief or loss. In fact, I rarely used the platform to post at all. I posted about my research and that I was hoping to speak with people who shared about their grief and loss on social media. Afterward, I received a direct message from Mike, who offered to share his story of losing both his grandfather and his best friend within the same year.

"Honestly, I'm always looking for any excuse to talk about them with anyone," he wrote. Before we spoke, Mike directed me to his Instagram profile where he shared about his best friend, Brian, and his grandfather. Scrolling through, I could catch myself up to speed as I read his stories and studied the photos he shared.

On his Instagram, he shared memories and remembrances of times that encapsulate the unique relationship he had with both his grandfather and Brian. I learned about his friendship with Brian; they loved planning get-togethers in advance, enjoying good food, and watching improv shows. In sharing about his grandfather's death, Mike expresses his sadness at those who did not get to know his grandfather personally. It makes me wish I knew him, myself.

Though it felt I already knew so much by the time we spoke, Mike began our conversation describing his grandfather, an introverted war veteran who regularly frequented his local YMCA. He talked about Brian, referencing the dinners together and outings I felt so familiar with. I addressed the Instagram posts and talked about how much I felt I learned even before we spoke. To this, Mike responded with something that stayed with me long after our conversation.

"There's a third person in this conversation, and that's the person you and I make together [...] and that third person is what I'm saying in these posts," he said. Having never heard this sentiment before, I listened closely as Mike explained what he meant by the third person. "It's different from who I am as an individual. And it's different from who you are as an individual. And that allows me to put my ego aside and serve it," he said.

Mike described his writing process for all of the posts about his grief as a stream of consciousness, hoping to capture his feelings in the moment as one might in a journal or in the Notes app of a phone. I can understand that in this process of sitting with his grief and how he feels about these relationships, he represents this third person in both losses. No one else has the exact stories and experiences he shares with his grandfather and with Brian. In losing them but honoring his memories in this way, he continues his relationship with them in a new way.

Mike shared with me that he spoke at Brian's funeral, at Brian's request. Among many people who spoke were other friends of Brian's who knew him from different walks of life. In these moments, Mike knew he wanted to best represent their relationship and the wide reach Brian had through his friendships.

Our conversation led me to consider our relationships are their own works of art, ones we share in different ways depending on how we express ourselves. Some people write poetry about being in love or photograph people they care about. Other people write letters or simply share remembrances between each other of favorite times together. Not only are these ways to stay connected, but also ways of celebrating the art of relating to each other.

When it comes to sharing moments of grief and loss on social media, I realize we might not just be asking to be seen for the pain we're in. We're being asked to be seen for ourselves.

Look at this love I feel for this person. Look at this love I had with this person.

What we know about grief and loss is that someone might no longer be with us physically, but the love we have for them does not go away. I've talked to many people about their grief who expressed their complete shock that life continues as it normally would after a loss. Cars still pass by on the street, dogs bark, emails arrive, and the sun still rises.

I think about how isolating it must be to use social media after a loss and want to feel connected to people somehow, only to feel like everything on social media also operates as it normally would. People share happy photos with friends and family, post birth announcements and photos of new apartments and houses—happy memories out and about.

It is common to see a brief post that acknowledges a loss. Whether someone shares on Facebook, Instagram, or another platform, it is one of many places where we can learn someone has passed. But what is less common are those moments of reflection, in missing someone we have lost or even someone we are in the process of losing. This is what I find so powerful in Mike's story: He keeps the memory of his loved ones alive in writing about them months beyond their passing.

Mike helped me realize we can share a more dynamic story of those in our lives beyond that of loss or grief. His work reminded me we can share the love we had with that person, the importance they held in our lives and their community, and the unique and special parts that make them who they are—the parts that make them irreplaceable.

My friend, Danielle, was twenty-three years old when she learned her mom had been diagnosed with stage four breast cancer. At the time, Danielle was preparing to move to North Carolina for a new job and was encouraged by her mom to pursue this next step, reassuring her everything would be okay despite her diagnosis.

The first year of this journey for Danielle and her mom, Peggy, was kept relatively private as they continued to figure out what would happen next and how to adjust to all the changes that came with Peggy's illness. When her mom went into remission for a brief period of time, Danielle thought things might be in the clear. But in early September 2019, Peggy had a seizure and Danielle decided to move home to care for her.

After this point, Danielle shared more about her mother's breast cancer on her Instagram page. She shared moments including Peggy's birthday, when Danielle bought her a makeover and she proudly posed for a photo where she could show she had eyebrows again. When things got really painful for Danielle, she chose not to share on social media because she worried the posts of her mother having mobility issues or difficulties after brain surgery would not be an accurate representation of who she is.

Danielle shared that, although she did show parts of her mom's experience of illness, she did not want that to be the only way she represented her mom on social media. She also chose to show Peggy enjoying a Dairy Queen Blizzard, playing with her dog, Joy, and opening the llama bucket hat Danielle gifted to her.

Danielle reflected on one photo she shared to Instagram while her mom was in the hospital after a major fall. In the photo, Peggy holds a Baby Yoda doll Danielle bought her from Target. "It's important to share this because this is where we're at. But it's still capturing the essence of my mom. Yeah, she's going but she's still here with her Baby Yoda," she told me.

I heard this several times in Danielle's story as she honored the memory of her mom, who passed away in September 2020. The idea of capturing Peggy's essence and sharing that, along with chronicling parts of her illness, held equal importance to Danielle. This way of presenting her story online shifts it from a narrow view of illness to a broader view of the love and relationship she and her mother shared.

It is easy to find traces of Peggy on Danielle's Instagram page now. Danielle, like Mike, is a powerful writer who has taken time and care to honor the memory of her mother. I think both Mike and Danielle's decisions to share and continue uplifting the memories of those they lost are part of a slow cultural shift on social media. They demonstrate a unique experience that can really only happen on social media, a visual and active archive of those we love. Of course, there are other archival spaces to capture the memories of those we have lost, but social media is the most common. It is a place where we can choose to represent those we love exactly as we remember them and exactly as they were.

I think of how many times in history people have been misrepresented in media. Social media has given us all a platform where we can portray ourselves and those around us how we choose. What it also does is allow people the ability to hold space for honoring those you have loved and cared about in your life if you choose to share about them on social media.

In this way, I think sharing our grief and loss adds to the mosaic of how we express ourselves on social media. Not only do we share the people who are important to us, but by showing how we relate to them, we can be seen for the love we shared. It is another way of honoring ourselves to present those pieces of our story and the connections that bring value and meaning to our lives.

When it comes to social media, I imagine everyone has different philosophies about what they choose to share and why. In general, people have different levels of privacy and what they are willing to put out into the world. Some choose to share on social media about the most specific parts of their daily lives while others keep at a further distance, sharing minimal information from time to time. This will continue. What I hope can change is that we have a cultural understanding of grief itself, in all its complexities. If people were open to understanding how grief moves with us, it could be a powerful tool for connection with others.

As David Kessler notes, his sixth stage of grief is to find meaning. Through finding meaning in the midst of loss, he believes he can sustain love as his life moves forward. Of the numerous ways we can find meaning, we might shift our perspective to realize writing about and capturing memories with loved ones brings immense meaning and purpose to people. The act itself, writing and sharing, in combination with the interaction social media spaces allow, can validate and uplift a grieving heart. Just like the act of love itself, sharing about someone who matters to you over time takes intention and action. It keeps our people close to us in new and valuable ways.

CHAPTER 8

HUMAN FIRST, PROFESSIONAL SECOND

During the 2021 Tokyo Olympics, four-time Olympic champion Simone Biles pulled out of the team final for women's artistic gymnastics. In a video explaining why she pulled out of the competition, Biles explained she was experiencing the "twisties": a common psychological phenomenon among gymnasts where one "loses air awareness and control of his or her body." Although she had no physical injuries when she pulled out of the competition, she explained her mental state led her to fear a potential injury. By choosing not to participate, she was protecting her physical and mental well-being.

I remember reading comments about people's reactions to Simone Biles's decision. While I admittedly barely follow sports, I pay close attention to mental health and how it's perceived in mainstream media, so this story stood out to me. Among positive comments of people expressing gratitude for Biles's bravery, there were criticisms as well. Texas Deputy Attorney General Aaron Reitz tweeted a video of Kerri Strug, who competed in the 1996 Olympics with an ankle injury.

He wrote, "Contrast this with our selfish, childish national embarrassment, Simone Biles." Strong reactions to his tweet led to a long apology and eventual deletion of the tweet itself.

As the story became more prevalent in news outlets, Simone Biles became more and more associated with mental health advocacy. By October 2021, Biles joined in partnership with Cerebral, a leading online mental health provider, as chief impact officer. She is also an investor in the company.

"At the end of the day, we're human, too, so we have to protect our mind and our body rather than just go out there and do what the world wants us to do," she told Athletes in Action. I consider what a risk Simone Biles took in her career and at such a young age.

Although we exist in a time where mental health has become more normalized in mainstream conversations, the backlash to her choice shows there is a long way to go. But in addition, it shows that before we are performers, colleagues, or anything else, we are human. To make a decision like the one she made shows there is a shift happening in which we can heal ourselves before we offer our gifts to the world.

A cultural value I've adapted to in my lifetime is that being too candid or open with colleagues could lead to consequences for my career. I remember my parents cautioning me about what I posted on my social media during college because it might prevent me from reaching my career goals. I know many people my age received the same messages from their parents at the time too. While I know they mostly referenced instances of teachers they knew who lost their jobs simply for posting pictures online with alcoholic beverages in their hands, I realize this message carried a heavier weight for me. I knew that to be able to achieve certain success, I would have to follow certain rules and observe what was okay and what was not.

My concern with this messaging of professionalism is that it lacks nuance, requiring us to represent ourselves as relatively one-dimensional people. While I clock out of my job at the end of the day, people like Simone Biles are even further pigeon-holed into one-dimensional roles because of the public eye. I believe this is why there was backlash to Biles' decision in the first place, because it indicated she might be more than an athlete we could rely on to represent the athleticism of our country. Potentially, she represents weakness in the eyes of those who think mental struggles are indicative of weakness.

I believe that Simone Biles's story can be applied to stories of grief and loss. I imagine some people have a strong reaction to the idea of sharing their experiences of grief and loss because it can feel unprofessional. Our society is heavily rooted in individualism and upward mobility, so struggling with mental health or grief is often seen at odds with what makes one professional and successful in their careers. Instead, these moments are considered weak or selfish rather than moments where we should lean into community.

There are other people who are changing this script without being directly involved in fields related to grief and loss, which means they are opening a door to deeper connection in wider professional spaces.

Laurie Kilmartin is a comedian and writer known for being a finalist on Last Comic Standing and a staff writer for Conan O'Brien. In 2014, her father was in hospice care after battling lung cancer. Laurie and her family spent his last days with him. One of the ways she documented the experience was to tweet about what was happening. She was supposed to perform stand-up during this time and remembers tweeting on a night when she wasn't on stage but was with her family instead.

"I wasn't intending to live-tweet when my dad died [...] I just started coming up with all these jokes that I would have told on stage that night," Laurie tells Michael Cruz Kayne in his podcast, *A Good Cry*. There are several tweets from this time period, mostly over the course of two days in February. These ones are particularly funny to me:

"Everyone copes their own way. I tweet, sister texts, while Mom shouts, 'I'M DOING A DARK LOAD, ANYONE GOT ANYTHING?'" -February 28, 2014

"Dad unknowingly unleashed a lifetime of nightmares on his 7 yo grandson w/these last words: 'I'll see you sooner than you think.'" -February 27, 2014.

Laurie remembers all the kind responses she received from people who offered their prayers to her father. She would then show the responses to her dad and said that they helped him a lot. Similar to her experience, Michael Cruz Kayne remembers when he once tweeted about losing his son shortly after he was born, he received nothing but positive and kind responses from people. As a comedian, receiving unanimous kindness from a large audience is a moment few and far between.

Comedy is one of many coping mechanisms that allows people to talk about pain in a relatable and funny way to others. But it can also be a mechanism for people to cover up their darker memories for the sake of entertaining people. I imagine a career as a comedian feels like a strange mixture of catharsis and incredible pressure. I like how Laurie took the time to connect with her skills as a comedian to document her experience with her dad, as it normalizes externalizing these moments to connect with others.

Although only some people become comedians, anyone can participate in social media. There are no qualifications or experience required to share your life on social media. Speaking candidly about painful or hard-to-swallow moments takes courage, but it also invites other people to do the same. I can appreciate that while a vast majority of Laurie's career centers on her knack for comedy, being able to combine that with more difficult experiences is a reminder that humor can exist even in the darkest of moments.

Comedy is a great space to test the limits of what we accept as normal in society. Many comedians push the limits and purposefully write their material to provoke a reaction from the audience or specifically pick at a cultural phenomenon that requires analysis. But what happens for those of us who do not have an audience or aren't in professional roles that elicit such positive feedback?

At the start of my research for this book, I posted on LinkedIn I was hoping to speak with people about their experiences of grief and loss and how they, if at all, opened up about it on social media. I received a direct message from a woman named Bernadette, who wanted to share her story.

Bernadette is an executive recruiter with over twenty-five years of experience in her field. When her brother finished his time in the military, he was unemployed and looking for jobs. Naturally, she hoped to be able to help. "He was so smart he walked into the SAT test room without a pencil, borrowed one, sat down, and finished early. He got a perfect score on each section. So very smart," she told me as she shared memories of them growing up together.

At the time her brother was looking for work, Bernadette shared he had otherwise been very successful in his career. He was smart and great with people. Dealing with unemployment for the first time in his life in his fifties, he did not want to accept the many offers of help from Bernadette or her husband. Unfortunately, Bernadette received a nightmare of a phone call one night from the local police department in her brother's town: he had taken his life.

Bernadette remembered how angry she felt when she processed this loss. "You're brilliant. You're handsome. You've got a sister in the business. You got a family that was willing to support you. But for whatever reason, you could not ask for help," she said.

At a certain point in her own grief, Bernadette had a realization there were probably more people just like her brother—people who were viewed as strong and competent, who were expected to have answers to problems they had not yet faced. She worried her brother never felt he could admit he needed help or was struggling and assumed there might be others like him out there who could use her support.

"That's why I started writing," she explained. Bernadette began sharing bits and pieces of her brother's story on LinkedIn and opening up her services to people who shared similar experiences with him. The more she shared, the more of a following she gained among the military community and men in general. While women would comment publicly on her posts, she often received direct messages from men about their stories of pain and despair. Now, she can contribute her years of experience in recruiting to a specific community she saw needed some attention.

Bernadette did clarify she was thoughtful and respectful about how she shared her brother's story, to maintain privacy for herself and anyone close to her family. Still, she knew it would be important to share his story so she could build rapport with others who might relate.

Bernadette's experience with loss directly translates to how she moved forward with her professional life after the death of her brother. Through her work, she has been able to help and empower others experiencing unemployment, something that can drastically affect one's sense of self beyond the financial implications. Her story also begs an important question when it comes to speaking on grief in professional spaces:

When we are quiet about our grief in these spaces, who benefits from the silence? When we are quiet about our grief in these spaces, who suffers in that silence?

Social media is one of the many spaces where we can leverage social connection through experiences that make us feel isolated. It offers a platform to those who do not already have large followings to still make an impact. Seeing each other engage in dialogue and support initiatives that benefit our collective healing can spread like wildfire.

Professionalism does not have to completely strip us of what makes us human. In fact, we can see in these examples that including more human sides of ourselves in our professional lives can have a direct and positive impact on people in their own careers. On a large scale, we see the impact of Simone Biles's decision has opened up more conversations about mental health. On smaller scales and with the use of social media, we see that invitations to discuss grief in professional spaces can help others find their way to themselves and each other.

CHAPTER 9

SOCIAL MEDIA AS MODERN DAY MOURNING GEAR

———

When Carolyn set off for a semester to study abroad in Yaoundé, Cameroon, she was excited to experience a new culture and environment. In a small group of six students from Dickinson College, she and her group members became a tight-knit family early on in the trip.

About a month into their time in Cameroon, all six students planned a trip together outside of the city. As they soon learned, planning these trips took longer than they were used to, so by the time they were ready to go they were understandably excited for the adventure ahead. On the day before they left, their English teacher took the group out for a meal together. Carolyn remembers that Legacy, one of the students on the trip, was often the one to be excited about trying new things and rally the group toward those new experiences. But on this particular day, she wasn't feeling great and went home after to rest. That night, the girls in the group all texted about what they planned to pack for the trip. It seemed like Legacy was back to normal.

The following day, everyone showed up at the student center where they had planned to meet before their trip. All were there except for Legacy. At first this didn't set off major alarms for anyone. Soon, Tiku, the program director, decided to visit the host family Legacy was staying with to see if everything was okay.

Roughly forty-five minutes after he left, Tiku returned to the student center with a look on his face that Carolyn still remembers today.

"Legacy is no more," he said to the group. At this time, everyone learned Legacy hadn't been feeling well again that morning and had been taken to the hospital. The heart of the issue was yet to be uncovered by the time Legacy passed away in the hospital.

Carolyn remembers the rest of that day as the longest day of her life. Attempting to process the shock of this loss in a foreign country, surrounded by people who only recently became like family to her, is understandably jarring. Being six hours ahead of the rest of the Dickinson community due to time zone differences also put the group in a strange, suspended limbo, while they waited for others to hear the news.

Carolyn and I were in the same graduating class at Dickinson and both studied abroad in the same semester when this happened. I remember receiving the email from our president telling us Legacy had died and sat in shock, trying to anticipate the impact of this loss on her family, the group that was with her in Cameroon, and our community as a whole.

Understandably, Legacy's passing shook the dynamic of the group in Cameroon. While some students chose to continue their time in Cameroon, Carolyn knew it was no longer the right choice for her to be there. Her anxiety increased as the days passed and she knew she couldn't be the healthiest version of herself if she stayed.

"The way they grieve in Cameroon is very different from American culture," she says. She was often told not to cry and that this was God's plan for Legacy, which felt dismissive of the grief and the tragedy of the situation.

It is important to acknowledge that different cultures may have vastly unique ways of processing grief. I fear rather than having rituals and traditions that help us grieve in the United States, we are only united in a grief process which demands we move on as quickly as possible. For those of us who are in moments of grief, how can we signal that to those around us? Can social media be a space that allows us to ask for space, comfort, or whatever we need at the time?

Carolyn was able to coordinate coming back to the US, rejoining campus, and taking summer classes so she could still graduate on time. Luckily, her welcome back to campus was one of warmth and comfort from her friends and faculty at the school who went out of their way to acknowledge what she had experienced. However, as the one student who returned to campus from the program, many people looked to Carolyn to talk about the experience and learn more about what happened. Talking about it was helpful for Carolyn, but it could be overwhelming at times.

She started posting on Instagram about how she was processing the experience and remembers one post that acknowledged how the healing process isn't linear. Her caption addressed those who told her she was weak for choosing to come home instead of staying in Cameroon. "I hope you come to understand that healing is a process, and all I'm trying to do is get through it," she said in the caption.

The comments were full of comforting and validating messages, reminding Carolyn she made the right choice and that people were glad to have her back. "It kind of made it easier for me to explain my feelings and where I was without having to directly talk to people about it," she answered when I asked how posting on social media helped her. "If I posted something and all of my closest friends saw it, it kind of just helped them understand where I was."

Though she was met with kindness back on campus, Carolyn still needed her own space to process. She remembered days that were incredibly difficult, where she returned to her room after a day of classes to cry. Posting on social media allowed her to communicate this process without needing to explain it on a daily basis, as she realized many people associated her with the tragedy she experienced in Cameroon.

Carolyn's Instagram is full of pictures of Legacy, as well as other photographs from her time in Cameroon with the rest of the group. I can tell there is a natural sense of closeness among those who were on the trip together, from the way they comment on Carolyn's posts and remind each other how much they love and miss being together. It is a visual archive, not just of her time with this group and their experience, but the unique connection they all share with each other.

To me, this story points out that one function of using social media to share about loss is to help us create a sense of awareness we might not have in other settings. It is a space where we can visually, in whatever way we choose, establish some sort of mourning process is happening in our lives. Through this, we can invite stronger connection with others who may relate or be curious to help us however they can.

Visual signs of mourning date back to times way before social media. For example, mourning attire has historically been one way to signal a loss. In earlier phases of its use during the Victorian era, people would wear mourning attire for months or even *years*. In 2014, social theorist Stacy Otto published a journal article in the *Journal of Social History* on mourning rituals. She studied how central mourning was to Victorian culture and how that changed in what she refers to as "post-Freudian, modern mourning rituals."

Otto states Victorians would make jewelry and flowers from their loved one's hair or save buttons from a dead soldier's uniform. In addition, Victorian women were "allocated much of the work of mourning." Widows would wear traditional mourning dress for up to two-and-a-half years. "Victorians were willing, moreover apt, to keep physical reminders of the one-lost, for objects of mourning functioned as relics that retained and represented something of the spirit of the departed," she notes (Otto, 2014).

It is clear mourning and honoring the dead were central parts of Victorian culture. So, what changed?

In the early 1900s, Sigmund Freud developed a theory that those who struggled to move on from death were "pathological, uncivilized, and neurotic." According to Otto, because of Freud's reach and the depth of his work, this theory made grief a taboo and made public mourning for long periods of time less socially accepted. After the death of his daughter in 1920, Freud backtracked on his theory, realizing his own grief persisted over nine years after his loss. At this point, though, it was too late and the cultural shift to move away from prolonged periods of mourning had already occurred (Otto, 2014).

Although conceptualized long ago, many of Freud's ideas still influence how people think about grief today. I am not surprised we now have a culture that begs people to move on from their grief as quickly as possible. Nora McInerny's 2018 TED Talk addresses how she experienced major losses within a short period of time: first, the loss of a pregnancy, followed by the death of both her father and then her husband, Aaron. One of the aspects she finds most upsetting about people's response to her loss is their expectation of how quickly she should move on. Nora remembers spreading Aaron's ashes in Minnesota after he died and realizing after she finished pouring them out there were remnants of his ashes on her hands. She licked them clean.

"I was so afraid of losing more than I had already lost and I was so desperate to make sure that he was always a part of me," she said.

What Nora shares points to a need of those in mourning often disallowed in our modern society: to remember their loved one and keep them close, rather than forget about them and move on. People tend to tiptoe around other's grief, assuming bringing up someone who passed away would make the grieving process more difficult. In reality, being able to talk about these losses and honor the people who held importance in our lives is what helps.

It is common for people to feel awkward engaging in conversations about grief or loss, especially when they can't relate to that experience firsthand. Some people choose to completely avoid the subject and others choose to dive in right away. As our needs are all different, the response we want from others will vary. If anything, social media allows people to connect with their community and ask for what they need.

I think of how Carolyn was able to continue sharing about her connection to Legacy and her pain throughout the experience of losing her. She could write freely about her experiences, knowing her close friends and family could see her posts and act accordingly. In sharing her story, she told me how healing it was to keep talking about what happened. She appreciated the way people knew she wanted to talk about Legacy based on how she shared her feelings online. It's also important to point out that social media was not the only method through which Carolyn found healing and community. Of course, her support system on campus helped her tremendously. That, in conjunction with her social media use, appears to me like a small team that worked together to help her express what she was going through and connect in ways that she needed to.

When we look at wider instances of sharing about our losses and healing processes, many people are quick to limit their understanding of them as attention-seeking. In these cases, it might be more effective to ask ourselves how it serves people to share their experiences on social media. Consider how it affects them and how the support of others might make the heaviness of their loss feel lighter in some way.

When someone experiences a big loss of some sort in their life, a sense of control is removed from their life—control over the circumstances, how others respond, of what is to come next. It can be incredibly overwhelming to process that feeling, but setting new boundaries and expectations can be empowering. Owning your narrative and sharing your story as you feel comfortable is important.

Here's another example.

When Michael Cruz Kayne's twin son died shortly after he was born, he and his wife had to experience the combination of grief and new parenthood all at once. While his employer at the time was incredibly understanding about the situation, encouraging Michael to take as much time off as he needed, he still remembers the struggle of returning to "normal life" after the loss.

"The hardest thing was not people telling me not to talk about it but more that I didn't want to have to tell anybody. I wanted them to already know. I could tell whenever I told someone that it was like punching them in the face." He recalled going into a comedy rehearsal when someone, in passing, asked him how his twins were doing. A question that might be so innocent to someone else, perhaps even striking a conversation about new parenthood, ended up being a horribly timed inquiry for Michael.

In that moment, his biggest concern was not wanting to ruin his colleague's day or having to deliver him bad news.

"I want to help [them] by preloading [their] brains with the information that this has happened [...] I don't want them to step on a landmine that they are not ready for," he said, jokingly, as a solution to the many situations like this he has been in. He then mentions how social media can serve as one solution to this dilemma, explaining how being able to share more widely about life experiences easily allows for people to be on the same page.

I can see how sharing about his son's death on social media, for example, would make the burden of Michael's grief just slightly lighter. In removing the necessity for him to deliver the horrible news to each person he interacts with, he knows people are aware of what he's been through and have been able to process it in some way on their own time. Not only does it serve Michael, but it also helps those who know and care about him by giving them an opportunity to process privately and show up as a support system in his life with strength.

In so many ways, our culture does not support people's need to grieve for long periods of time. Bereavement leave for most employees is painfully short and people generally expect those in mourning to return to normalcy as soon as possible. While we no longer don the Victorian-era mourning apparel, we know people grieve long after they experience a loss.

What can be challenging about these times is how mourners are forced to communicate about the loss or never asked to share about it at all.

Social media can act as a visual aid to help people understand someone is in the midst of a loss. It allows people the agency to communicate about their needs and ask for help or space, depending on where they are with the process—a simple "please ask" or "don't ask," or something in between to let others know, "I have lost. I am lost."

CHAPTER 10

BECOMING THE SPECTACLE: WHAT WE CAN LEARN FROM INTERACTING WITH GRIEF

In 1974, Serbian performance artist Marina Abramović created one of her most well-known pieces of performance art, *Rhythm 0*. On a table in front of her were seventy-two objects that all varied in nature and function. In front of her were grapes, bread, roses, and perfume as well as scissors, nails, and a pistol loaded with one bullet.

"I am an object. You can do whatever you want to do with me. I will take all responsibility for six hours," was written on the table.

Recounting what happened during the six hours, Abramović states that at first the public was almost shy to interact with her. They would look at her, hand her a rose, or give her a kiss.

But slowly, they became more "wild," she described. People poked rose thorns into her skin and gave her cuts. One person positioned the gun in Abramović's hand and pointed at her neck as if she would pull the trigger.

When the six hours ended, an employee at the gallery announced time was up. Abramović began to move toward the public. Immediately, everyone started running.

"People actually could not confront me, myself, as a person," she said.

A *Guardian* article covering Abramović's career commented about *Rhythm 0*, "When she invited the public to use those objects on her frozen figure, Abramović exposed a savagery lurking beneath the surface of otherwise civilized human beings." This piece of work, among many thought-provoking works Abramović created, is unsettling in what it uncovers about human interaction. When they knew she could not retaliate, the public interacted with Abramović, with both intimacy and violence. When they knew she could potentially retaliate, the public reacted with fear.

Now, almost fifty years after Abramović performed the piece, I see real applications of the same lack of ability to acknowledge each other's personhood.

In a digital era, we have become even more comfortable with reducing each other down to what we can comprehend, compartmentalizing what does not add up, and normalizing judgments at each other along the way. Can we look at these interactions on social media in the same way an art critic would view Abramović's work?

Prior to creating *Rhythm 0*, Abramović admitted she had become frustrated with the constant criticism of performance art. People did not understand performance art nor did they consider it a valid form of expression compared to other art forms. While *Rhythm 0* has many interpretations, it shows more about the people who interacted with it than Abramović herself.

In the same vein, there is currently no consensus on how social media could or should be interpreted. However, dismissing social media as trivial largely neglects the ways these platforms allow us to learn about and analyze human behavior. Just like in *Rhythm 0* where we saw impulses toward intimacy and violence, what can we uncover about how we interact with each other's grief on social media? What can we learn about what we currently accept in conversations of grief and what we still collectively reject?

As I started to research grief on social media, I noticed the algorithm on my TikTok account cater to my interests more and more. As I mentioned in chapter five, the way the TikTok algorithm works is particularly accurate and reflective of the content the user engages with. Every video I would scroll by that addressed grief of some sort sparked my interest. Not only would I watch and analyze, but I would also spend time scrolling through comments on the video to see how people reacted.

Grief is a very personal experience. However, when it is made public, it invites people like myself to be a bystander or collaborator, if I choose. But instead of grapes, roses, or scissors in my hands, I am invited to use my words—any words.

I opened TikTok one day and came across a video of an older man who goes by Grandpa Beppa. I don't follow him on TikTok and had never seen him before but assumed his content would resonate with me somehow due to the algorithm.

In the video I watched, I notice Grandpa Beppa's round glasses and the white tufts of hair that surround his head like a crown. He looks into the camera, smiling. The words on the screen say: "I took a picture of my wife, every time she looked beautiful this week." I sit and wait to see a picture of a woman his age, perhaps with the same makeup look I have watched my grandmother do since I was a little girl. What follows, instead, are six photos of sunsets. I realize my assumption was wrong. He grieves his wife and sees her in the sunsets each day. The video has over eighteen million likes and more than 300,000 comments. It has been shared almost 450,000 times.

As tears welled up in my eyes, I opened the comment section to feel a sense of connection with others who likely shared the same feelings. The top comment read: "U took pictures of the world; she was your world." Grandpa Beppa liked this comment and responded with three heart emojis. There were one million likes on the comment itself and a thread of a couple thousand comments underneath.

I continued reading more comments from people who shared the video made them cry or "hit them in the feels." Some wrote they "weren't ready" for this type of content so early in their day. People told Grandpa Beppa his wife looked beautiful and some of them referred to him as Grandpa, though I can only assume most who do this do not know him personally.

I clicked on his profile and saw his bio states he loves us all and has over 600,000 grandchildren. His bio also says to follow along to be part of the family. I see he posts videos with his granddaughter, often following popular trends I have seen on TikTok.

Grandpa Beppa's video resonated deeply with the audience it reached. People felt sympathy and empathy for his story and I can only assume his age and the sweetness in his face made people more inclined to engage and show him support. While I did not sift through all 300,000+ comments, I struggled to find any negative remarks from anyone at the several glances I had taken.

On another day, I scrolled through my feed again and came across another video of grief, but this time from a young influencer I had seen before. Her name is Suede Brooks and I saw her first on TikTok but learned she gained a platform from starting a YouTube channel in her preteen years. Her content primarily focuses on lifestyle, showing vacations and "day in the life" vlog-type videos. Brands pay Suede to try on their clothes, so she brings enthusiasm to her videos to entice others to purchase sleek dresses, trendy jewelry, and cheeky bikinis.

Most TikToks I see of Suede are "get ready with me" videos, in which she yells "hi guys!" while in a bra and underwear, usually with an iced coffee in hand. She proceeds to show what she will wear for the day and ends the videos by wishing everyone a great day. So, when Suede's newest video appeared on my feed, I realized I had not seen a video from her in a while, but I learned why right away.

As she lays on her bed wearing a small white tank top, with her silky hair sprawled around her and a diamond necklace around her neck, the overlay of text says: "Lost my father very suddenly a few months ago." The sound in the background is called "Pope is a Rockstar" by Sales. A popular trend on TikTok at the time was to use this sound in a video congratulating oneself for a major achievement or a moment of growth. Using the sound indicated someone was planning on sharing that moment about themselves or someone else, but the lyrics were misinterpreted to say, "Go little rockstar".

Following the announcement of Suede's father passing was a video of Suede in front of a large painting of a man I could only assume was her father in his younger years. The painting is in hues of yellow and her father has sunglasses and a hat on as he smiles with his mouth wide open, as if in the middle of a laugh or a story. "My brother surprised me with this painting he made, now I know he is watching my every move," Suede's caption read on the video. Now, in sweatpants and a sweatshirt in this video, she glances back at the painting, smiling as the words "go little rockstar" play in the audio. Like I did with Grandpa Beppa's video, I scrolled through the comments on Suede's video as well.

Selfishly, I wondered if there was more information on her father's passing, but I also was curious to know how people responded to her video. Like other videos I'd seen about loss, hers included many comments extending sympathy to Suede for her loss. One comment caught my attention: "Who thirst traps and captions it 'lost my father very sudden a few months ago?' Like, yes girl smize for your dead father. Morbid behavior."

I was not entirely surprised to see someone had commented this. In a world full of judgment and projection, many people unfortunately respond to these posts with criticism. In processing this moment, I also realized it was one negative comment among hundreds of support and I could easily ignore it.

I put myself in Suede's position instead, considering in this moment she might actually read through every single comment. I think I would.

I wonder if we, as a society, are only comfortable with grief if it is palatable to us. If an elderly man who lost his wife shares a photo of sunsets in remembrance of her, we accept this reality and allow it to bring us closer to our empathy and humanity. We can accept that a young woman like Suede has built a career off influencing others in terms of their lifestyle and their purchases. Seeing videos and photos of her body on a daily basis is part of the job. Anyone who follows her becomes familiar with seeing her body, but when she shows it in the context of grief, her body is sexualized and her grief is minimized.

Grandpa Beppa and Suede both made themselves vulnerable in their own ways by sharing their grief. In doing so, they opened up a space for criticism, commiseration, and anything in between. I imagine they both knew these reactions were possible, regardless of what they shared, and I will never know the precise reason they still chose to publicly share their experiences. I think it is common for people to want to share and universalize hardships others can relate to.

I recognize many people find it easier to act cruel toward others online than in real life.

This is similar to how cruelty came easily to those who were handed weapons in front of a woman who could not fight back. In its time, Maria Abromović's experiment was not widely understood. Why would she welcome violence if she could avoid it? Was it to feel alive? Was it with the intention of being hurt in the end?

Now, those who choose to share about grief online tend to be met with mixed reviews from those who gather to view the spectacle of it all. As I scroll through comment sections of videos and posts, I can almost visualize who holds what items in their hands. Who offers something to help and who comes toward others with violence? Do others' responses really say anything about the person who sits, defenseless? Have we considered that we point fingers in the wrong direction?

When we criticize each other's expression of grief, what we are actually saying is we do not give ourselves permission to grieve that way. Or, we cannot imagine we might someday experience that feeling.

We need to share with each other because we need to grow together.

PART TWO

INTRODUCTION: A GRIEVER'S UTOPIA

"To be hopeful in bad times is based on the fact that human history is not only of cruelty, but also of compassion, sacrifice, courage, and kindness. If we see only the worst, it destroys our capacity to do something. If we remember those times and places where people have behaved magnificently, this gives us the energy to act. And if we do act, in however small a way, we don't have to wait for some grand utopian future. The future is an infinite succession of presents, and to live now as we think human beings should live, in defiance of all that is bad around us, is itself a marvelous victory"

-HOWARD ZINN

When I graduated college, a friend I met through the women's and gender studies department gifted me a book called *The Feminist Utopia Project*. The book is a collection of over fifty essays from powerful feminist voices on what the future could look like in a Feminist Utopia. After learning so many complexities about gender and its intersections with race and class, I left college with a fire in my belly to change the world. I leaned on powerful theorists and activists like bell hooks, Kimberlé Crenshaw, and Audre Lorde to guide my way. I had my own visions of what the future could look like, but diving into the creative essays in *The Feminist Utopia Project* brought me even more hope and excitement for what intersectional feminism could bring to the world.

I love the idea that on the other side of pain is hope. As someone who deeply cares about many social causes, I have learned activism without hope is empty and without love for the people whose lives we hope to change. I think about how many people are grieving in their own ways and I envision a world where we support that grief process more than we do now.

I know I cannot change all the factors that contribute to why anyone experiences grief in the first place—I wish I could bring people back or prevent their illnesses. But I know that isn't possible.

I do think there is plenty of space for hope and dreaming when it comes to how we can envision the future of social media use, grief and loss, and our own positions in those spaces. While the term "grievers' utopia" feels like an oxymoron, I do think there are worlds of improvement we can make in our daily lives to support the grieving process for those around us.

The following section is a series of creative essays I have written to spark thoughts and feelings about this future. These stories and characters are completely made up but some are inspired by interviews I have done and bigger questions about the root causes of problems we see today on social media. I hope you will see parts of yourselves in the characters I've created and recognize the humanity in how they deal with their dilemmas.

There is no right answer to the choices that anyone makes, but I hope to illustrate some of the nuances of their decisions and, by doing so, invite you to consider them as well.

Each essay begins with a short introduction of what I hope to accomplish and illustrate in the piece, to center you into the story and where you are. I hope these stories open us up to the possibility that the experience of grief and our interactions with social media and technology do not need to stand at odds with each other. I have considered that some people's fear of increased use of technology means technology would replace human interaction and what we deem sacred of our interpersonal relationships.

In this final section of the book, I acknowledge there is no replacement for that sense of connection. However, technology can facilitate and help others understand this connection if we allow ourselves to analyze and interpret in that way. Can we use these tools to drive connection rather than division?

Are there solutions we have not yet tried that would help us move through grief together?

CHAPTER 11

INFLUENCER THERAPIST

In February 2022, leading psychiatrist and brain expert Dr. Daniel Amen joined as a guest speaker on one of my favorite podcasts, *Girls Gotta Eat*. After discussing the various brain types and recommending foods to aid people's happiness levels, Dr. Amen spoke briefly about some of his celebrity clients. Justin Bieber and Miley Cyrus were among a couple he mentioned. His comments reignited a fascination I have with mental health support for those who predominantly exist in the public eye.

This fictional piece puts in conversation two interviews I did in the early phases of research for this book. I spoke to a woman named Alex who has spent over ten years of her career in influencer marketing. In 2010 she had over a million followers on Pinterest and continued to build on her brand and lifestyle content, working with companies like Target, Home Depot, and Anthropology. When we spoke, she told me about her life in Arizona as a single mom and how she chose to share about her divorce on Instagram when it happened.

Kelly is an integrative counselor and consultant who practices in Arizona. She agreed to let me ask her some questions about social media as a theme in her practice. Her presence, insightfulness, and creativity are central to what makes her so successful. The coincidence of Kelly and Alex's location and what I learned from them both inspired me to write this piece. While there are no direct quotes from either Kelly's or Alex's interviews in this essay, I am emulating the advice and experiences they shared with me.

When I interviewed Alex, she shared with me she was ready to move on from sharing about her grief. I wanted to take that feeling and contextualize it with her grief experience, pulling out some of the feelings as they are prompted by Kelly in the story.

Through this therapy session, I hope to illustrate there are many emotions wrapped up in how we choose to share our lives. This is exacerbated by Alex's status as someone with a large following, but it can be applied to anyone who chooses to share their life online in a more personal sense. Additionally, I hope this invites more compassion and understanding when we jump to judgment of what is "too much" to share. If it helps our community or creates community in the first place, could we see the positive side of that sharing?

"I've confirmed with Alex that she's okay with you listening to our session today. It's only our third session so it should be easy to get caught up," Kelly tells me as we step into her office. It's beautifully decorated with handwoven rugs and pillows on the floor and a single couch, but it looks stiff. In the corner there is a small desk, but I get the sense she doesn't use it often.

Kelly wears flared black jeans, a T-shirt, and large, eclectic accessories. I can see some of her tattoos, one of which takes up a large portion of her right wrist. She moves comfortably, with ease and care.

"Where should I, er, sit?"

"Oh, I always sit on the floor. Is that okay? I find it helps me connect more," says Kelly.

"Of course," I say. I can already tell I like her approach. She has a warmth about her I instantly connect with. Kelly goes over to the small sink in her office and pours water into a watering can. I look around and notice all the plants that scatter the room, while Kelly makes her rounds, watering the plants and humming under her breath.

I chose to shadow Kelly because she primarily works with influencers. Admittedly, I've always wanted to hear what these sessions might sound like but I'm not sure if it could ever be my specialty. I have a few friends minoring in influencer studies in my program though. I can't wait to tell them about today.

I hear a knock at the door and in walks Alex.

"Hi Kelly," she says in a sweet, soft voice. She looks at me and smiles. As she walks toward me, I notice how small she is. I looked her up on Instagram before coming into the session but for some reason, in my mind, she was seven feet tall. Her olive-toned skin and frizzy, beautiful hair catches my eye; it looks as if she isn't wearing any makeup at all.

"Have a seat," Kelly says. Gesturing at me, "This is Maura; she'll be observing today. Is that still alright?"

"Sure, yeah. Hi Maura," she says. I say hello and sit by a small pile of pillows nearest Kelly. Nervously, I pull at my blouse and wait for Kelly and Alex to situate themselves.

Kelly sits comfortably on a donut-shaped pillow on the floor. She takes a deep breath, smiles at me, and focuses her attention on Alex.

"Alex. How are you?"

"I'm okay," Alex replies. "I'm okay," she says again, nodding.

"Wonderful. I wanted to root us today in where we ended in our conversation last week. You were saying you wanted to make some changes in how you share about your life. Is that something you want to keep exploring?"

"Yes. I think this shift is what I need right now. I don't want to be consumed anymore. I just want to be me," Alex says.

I feel like I've been let in on a secret by accident, because I know what Alex is talking about without having been at either of her previous sessions with Kelly. On Instagram, she recently shared a post about unfollowing therapists and no longer listening to advice podcasts. She shared about how she didn't want to be known for overcoming and healing anymore.

"Mmm," Kelly says. It's a deep, knowing sentiment. "Say more."

"I'm glad I shared so much of my life—it kept me going; it kept me *sane*. In a way, I guess, it gave me purpose. But I feel like I've healed so much at this point, I wonder when I stop looking at myself as a work in progress and just live my life."

Kelly nods.

After a brief pause, she asks, "When did you become a work in progress?"

"Maybe always…" Alex begins, "I guess that would make sense. The idea that I can improve myself and my life all on my own has always impacted me. It's why I gained so much success online in the first place. I chose when and where, you know? It was all up to me. But then when he cheated—my ex-husband, I mean." She turns to me, making sure I know who she's referring to. I thankfully nod at her, as if I am learning this information for the first time—as if I hadn't read every post or clung to her every word, on my own.

"When he cheated, I became a work in progress but in the worst way. Like I could see everything I hated about myself all at once—all the shame, all the fear. I guess sharing it all made it feel less awful. Like, I realized I wasn't the first person to feel this way, and I won't be the last," she says.

"That makes a lot of sense," Kelly says. "The work that was once empowering, for you, became the opposite. What does it look like now?"

"I guess I'll always be somewhat of a work in progress. Nobody ever stops evolving. I think what it looks like now is... hm," she pauses for a while. I'm almost shocked when I notice she's closed her eyes and she's taking a deep breath, as if we just arrived at the ocean and she needs to savor the scent.

"I want to live, freely. I want to write and share. I want to be known and loved for who I am, beyond what I've been through. I want to show other people that this part exists, too," she says.

"What is 'this part?'" Kelly asks.

"The other side of grief, I guess. Accepting what has happened to get me here. It was so painful... I wouldn't wish it on anyone. But I love who I am now. I hope they'll accept me for it too. I guess I'm scared they won't," she says.

Her expression shifts so quickly with this thought. I'm nervous I've been staring at her too much but, admittedly, I'm captivated by her honesty. I'm not sure what I was expecting.

"When you first started sharing about your grief journey, what happened? To your online presence, I mean," Kelly asks.

"I was so scared. I knew it was a risk—all that I'd built could disappear. Some people left, but some people stayed. I think the numbers meant less to me; I knew I was creating something more authentic. I chose to focus on that."

"This fear you have now, is it the same as before?" Kelly asks.

"I'm not sure. I guess it's different in a way. Some people are known for their joy but rejected for their pain. It's almost as if I've been living in the inverse. Is my joy authentic now? Is it allowed?"

"What do you think?" Kelly asks. I notice how focused she is.

"I mean I know it's allowed. I know that. But I haven't always *felt* it. That my joy can be authentic, that I can live differently. I wonder if, in a way, my pain kept me protected."

Kelly's eyes widen and she nods emphatically. She leaves silence, which I respect. I'm not great at that part.

"I remember being so scared that nobody would want to work with me anymore and nobody would understand. And some of that was true, but more of what I saw was a stronger connection. It felt intoxicating! I didn't have to be alone. I tear up just thinking of the possibility that I've helped anyone else understand their pain and what this loss feels like. But it's also not all of who I am. I know that."

"Do you often look back on the pieces you've shared on your social media?" Kelly asks.

"Yeah, not as often as I used to, but I still do," Alex says.

"What do you see?"

"When I was a kid, I kept a journal. I liked looking back and reading... I'd remember things I'd completely wiped out of my memory. In a way, this feels sort of like that. But it's as if I'd passed the journal around and let people write with pencil in the margins," she says.

Kelly nods.

"I guess," Alex continues, "I guess it's sort of beautiful. Occasionally I've felt like, maybe it's all too much to have shown anyone. But then I think, I might have done this alone. And that would have been so hard. I can always look at the margins now and know I was never alone."

"I think that's amazing. And empowering," Kelly says.

After Alex's session, Kelly sits with me and lets me ask questions.

"What did you think, Maura? What stands out to you from that session?" she asks me.

"I don't know. I'm sort of fascinated by Alex. I like the metaphor she made about journaling... I've never really considered how that can change one's experience. Do you think it's right for her to have shared all that she did?" I ask.

Kelly pauses.

"My job isn't really to determine if it's right or not to share like that. Because in reality, I don't know. My goal is to focus on the well-being of that individual and make sure that sharing serves *them*. Not everyone is like Alex. But personally, I think she's done something incredible. It makes me think about what life would be like if nobody spoke up," she says.

She looks so serious when she says this, it makes me want to know much more about her than I probably ever will.

"I feel sort of embarrassed to admit this, but I really didn't think this field had the depth that other ones do. I mean, I guess I've just considered so much of this to be superficial—about appearances," I say.

"You certainly aren't the first or the last to say that!" Kelly laughs. "You know, I don't blame you for thinking that way. I think a lot of people do. And I used to, too! But I think of social media like a mirror—you see what you want to see. It's a microcosm of our lives—we can't pretend it isn't there like people might want to do. The reflection you're doing right now is what I wish more people would do. I think it would solve a lot of problems," she says.

CHAPTER 12

GRIEFCHAT

In a culture that is still uncomfortable with the emotions and longevity of grief, are there new technologies that can support grievers?

In chapter five, I mentioned a girl named Carson who shared on TikTok about losing both of her parents within the same year. Carson talked about how her choice to share partly came from feeling like she was a burden on her close friends and family. This essay is meant to illustrate a solution where the main objective for two grievers is to share their experience in a fixed time and space with each other using a new social networking platform.

The emphasis is not so much on the furthering of a relationship, but more on the present moment of how we sit with each other in grief. While GriefChat is not an entirely anonymous platform, as you will learn, the concept behind it suggests grief is a universal experience that does not need to be handled alone or even only with those closest to you. Healing can happen in unique spaces that might not only help but also expand our ability to connect with one another when we step outside of our comfort zones.

You will notice that Bethany, the protagonist in this story, is given statistics on grief in her area as they pertain to race, class, and gender. In my vision for the future, I wonder if this information would help us find powerful connections with people, wherever we are.

As I wrote, I began to wonder what these statistics would look like in my hometown if I had them. Would they help?

I'm about to close Instagram after an hour of mindlessly scrolling through my feed when I realize I have an unread message request. I see it begins with, "Hi Bethany! I noticed your profile..." Great, another strange request to be a brand representative. I open the message and am about to click the delete button when the word "grief" catches my eye.

I read the full message.

"Hi Bethany! I noticed your profile because of your use of the #grief hashtag. I hope you don't mind me reaching out. Our company has developed a new technology called GriefChat and we are looking for people willing to test it out. We're reviving the technology from Chat Roulette (remember those days?) but using it as a way to connect people going through grief. Would you be interested in testing it out? Message me for more details!"

I read the message a second and third time to make sure I understood correctly. I remember sleepovers with my friends when I was younger when we'd go on Chat Roulette and talk all night with people we didn't know. It seems strange Sthat there would be a new rendition of this, but for grievers.

I instantly picture the format of Chat Roulette, flipping from one person to the next, but each screen is just another person crying. God, that sounds depressing.

I decide to click on the GriefChat profile and see they only have a few posts at this point—seventeen, to be exact. The first nine constitute a larger spread of posts that connect together like a puzzle. It's of a map of the United States and resembles one of those maps used to track the concentration of an illness depending on location. I assume instead of an illness, they track grief.

In the bio, I see a link to a website and follow it. The landing page for GriefChat is a video of an older woman with long salt-and-pepper hair and soft brown eyes. I click play.

"Hi. I'm Dana. Three years ago, my eleven-year-old son died from leukemia. His name is Nathan. He loved riding his bike and searching for caterpillars outside. I miss him every day." Dana pauses and I assume she's picturing Nathan in her mind. Her voice is low and smooth. "I thought I would never stop hurting, and to be honest, I still hurt every day. But I never knew how isolating this grief would be. With my friends and my siblings who all have healthy, living children, I feel out of place sometimes. I've searched for others like myself, but couldn't seem to form the connection I was looking for. That's until I started using GriefChat."

The screen changes and I see a woman walking toward the camera wearing a sage green pantsuit. I recognize her as the woman who sent me the initial message. "GriefChat combines the technology used in the old Chat Roulette site with what's working on dating apps. By filling out a simple survey about your grief, we connect you with those in your area whose responses are most like yours. You choose when you chat, and you eliminate anyone you don't like and you never have to see them again. Simple as that!" she says.

I audibly snort at the part where she mentions 'what's working on dating apps,' thinking of how fed up I've been lately trying to date. According to my logic, nothing about them works that well. I decide to click the link to sign up for the free trial.

Before I begin, I get up from my desk and shut my bedroom door. I'm not really sure why; I guess the whole thing feels sort of strange. I've adapted to almost every facet of modern technology at this point, but the idea of hopping on a video call with a stranger and bonding over grief is still a bit out of reach.

It feels so intimate.

After I fill out the usual fields—name, age, gender—I begin to fill out a survey. The first question reads: *Are you grieving the death of a loved one? Yes or No.*

I click yes, but wonder what person would click no. I thought grief only applied to someone dying. Maybe I'm wrong. I am new to this whole thing, to be fair.

Who was that person to you? My mom.

How long ago did she die? Six months ago.

On a scale of 1-10, 1 being completely misunderstood and 10 being totally understood, how much do the people in your day-to-day life understand your grief process? 2

I go on to answer several more questions of this nature, which get a better sense of my grief and what it feels like on a day-to-day basis. The space for that question isn't large enough for me to say: *it feels like every day I fall into a hole and people see me falling but don't do anything about it, and I can't do anything about it. so eventually I just resort to giving up, or crying, or absolute nothingness.*

"Insurmountable" is what I decide on.

The final questions give me pause. *Are you single?* Yes.

Why would they need to know this?

Do you feel your grieving process has made it harder to connect with someone romantically? Obviously yes. This question reminds me of my most recent date, which immediately makes me cringe.

A perfectly nice, normal guy asked me, "So what are your parents like?" I froze and didn't know how to answer. It's so awkward seeing someone's reaction when you inevitably have to say, "Well, my dad's not around... and my mom just died. So, yeah, tell me about your parents?"

The final question of the survey asks if they can connect Grief-Chat to my Hinge account, the same way Google will ask if they can access your location or save your credit card on file. There's an asterisk under this question: *We believe that the types of people you are interested in dating might have some relevance to who you'd connect with most. This is NOT a dating app of any sort, but the technology used on dating apps has been determined as a helpful part of the process for us.

I click allow, and then continue.

"Welcome, Bethany," is written in sage green on what I now assume is my personal home page. In the top right corner of the page is where my profile exists, listing all my survey responses and offering options to change any of them. Underneath the welcome sign is a button that says, "My survey results" and I click on it.

"Bethany, we found over 250 people within a ten-mile radius of you who are also grieving the death of a parent within the last year." This is so strange. It feels like I'm clicking through my Spotify Wrapped, but it's about grief! I realize I'm meant to swipe through the pages, so I click to the next. "Of these 250 people, 13 percent are within your age group of eighteen to twenty-five. Sixty percent are also women, and 20 percent of these people also identify as mixed-race, like you."

Reading this line makes me feel excited. I continue to see one of those large word collages with tons of tiny words compacted into the shape of letters that spell out "Grief." I see a large "insurmountable" written in the center of the E and remember writing this. "Here is how others in your age group and demographic have described their grief. We have saved this graphic in your personal profile for reference, as well."

I look at the other words. *A black hole. Nothingness. Everything. Overwhelming. Debilitating.* I make a mental note to come back to this page at a later date. I click through to the next slide.

"Ready to meet?" is all it says. I click "Yes."

I'm prompted by my browser to allow video and audio for the platform and see my screen looks almost exactly like Chat Roulette when I was younger. I can see myself in the top screen while another screen below me is just black. On the left, though, is a list that reminds me of an AOL chatroom. I can see there are 250 people in my "queue" and that 152 of them are currently active on the platform. I can't imagine speaking to all 250 people. Am I supposed to?

On the right-hand side of the screen I notice a chat pop up, similar to a customer service chat.

"Hi Bethany, I'm Matt. Welcome to your virtual landing room. You can sit here for however long you need, and there is no pressure to talk to anyone yet. We know this can be overwhelming! How are you doing?"

"A little nervous, I guess. Am I supposed to talk to all these people?" I respond.

"No, of course not! You can talk to whomever you like. Just click 'Start' when you're ready. You'll be connected to one person to begin with. If you aren't comfortable talking to them, simply click 'End Session' and a message will come up letting you know the session is being terminated. You don't have to carry on a conversation with anyone you don't enjoy speaking with. This is for you, use the platform as you'd like."

"What if something creepy happens?" I ask nervously, remembering horror stories from Chat Roulette.

"Great question. We've implemented several safety measures for the platform. The 'End Session' button is always there for you to use, but we also have a 24/7 chat and hotline to report any misdemeanors. So far, we have not had any reports of poor behavior."

"Okay. I think I'm ready!" I type.

"Great! We're here if you need us."

I click "Start" in the top right corner and see the chat automatically minimizes and what I've decided to call the "friends" list on the left does as well. The screen below mine has a white circle that is moving, indicating the service is loading.

Soon, I see the face of a girl pop up on the screen below mine. Her screen says "Jade." She has curly black hair and big brown eyes. She looks kind.

"Hi Jade," I say.

"Hi Bethany! Do you go by 'Bethany' or 'Beth?'" she asks. I get this a lot.

"Beth is cool with me! It's nice to meet you. I'm not really sure what we're supposed to do now…" I say, trailing off awkwardly.

"Yeah, nice to meet you, too! Oh, don't worry, just give it a second. We have some time for intros but then—" she starts but is interrupted by a voice.

"Welcome, Jade and Bethany. Now that you've introduced yourselves, you can choose to get to know each other how you'd like, or you can start by picking a question from the deck of cards. We know talking about grief can be difficult, so go at your pace and do what feels comfortable," says a voice that sounds exactly like the one from the demo video. The transcription of her words appear in the center of our two screens.

"Okay if I pick a card? I'm not great at small talk," I admit.

"Yeah, go for it. I've been doing this for a little while and the questions are actually pretty cool," Jade says. I notice in her hands she's playing with Silly Putty.

"Oh my god, I used to play with Silly Putty all the time! They still make that?" I laugh.

"Oh yeah. It helps me when I'm anxious," she says.

"Making a mental note to get some for myself after this. Okay, I'm clicking the card deck," I tell her.

When I click the card deck, a visual pops up on the screen, blurring mine and Jade's videos momentarily.

> **Card 1: Finding Common Ground**
>
> **Jade and Carolyn: You both lost your moms in March of 2019.**
>
> **Jade's mom died from a sudden heart attack.**
>
> **Bethany's mom died from a car accident.**

I'm amazed at how quickly our responses were put into this format. I picture Jade filling out the same survey I just submitted and I wonder if she struggled with any of the questions I did. I wonder if the dating profile questions were just as absurd to her.

I hear Jade mumble, "Sheesh, you too. God, I'm sorry," and it snaps me back to the current moment.

I click "next" on the card.

> **Share with each other a favorite memory of your mother. Take as much time as you'd like.**

I can't remember the last time anyone asked me this. I think about her every day, but most of my conversations with people tend to circulate around if I'm doing okay and how school is going—really anything that would keep them from the awkwardness of talking about Mom and how much it hurts.

"Do you want to start?" I offer to Jade.

"Nah, you. I think I need a minute to think," she says.

"Okay. Yeah, I can go. It's kind of stupid, though," I say.

"Impossible. I'm not judging," says Jade. This is so weird. It feels like we know each other.

"Well, my mom and I used to make egg rolls together. Neither of us can cook, but we watched a cooking show once where someone made it look so easy. So we went to the store and got what we'd need: cabbage, carrots, tofu, and those little wonton things. I was probably only ten or eleven when we started, so I couldn't even reach the kitchen island to help her make the mixture." The picture that pops in my head from the memory makes me smile a bit.

"She pulled a chair up and let me stand on it while we sliced vegetables and prepared the mix. I got really good at folding and rolling the egg rolls, so that was always my job. Then she'd go fry them out in the garage and bring them back inside. They were so good. I think we made them every month together while I was still living at home. And when I'd come back to visit from college, it was, like, understood we'd make them together."

"I love that. Is there a particular time you made egg rolls together that stands out to you?" Jade asks. The question makes me feel really warm—seen, I guess.

"Yes, actually—when I got accepted to college. I ran downstairs to tell her and she was so excited, she said we had to celebrate. We made eighty-five egg rolls and invited some of my friends over to share with us. It was so ridiculous; we didn't even cook anything else. We just sat on the living room floor with a group of us, eating egg rolls and talking about how exciting college would be. I loved that," I say.

"Wow. That's pretty cool. I'm glad you have a memory like that. Have you made egg rolls since she died?"

"No. I'm scared to. I'm worried it will be too much, like just the smell of the fryer oil or something would make me feel awful. I don't know... I'll get there. What's your memory?" I ask, hoping to change the subject.

"This was a hard one, actually. I wasn't super close with my mom. She worked a lot. She was a lawyer—a badass. But honestly, I didn't see her a ton. But my favorite memory of her was watching her do her makeup. I usually wouldn't catch her in the morning before work, but sometimes she'd go into the office on Saturdays and I'd sit with her then. She had a really specific routine, and she'd always have a hot espresso next to her while she did it all. I thought she was so beautiful," Jade says.

"That's such a cool memory to have. I feel like it's a rite of passage to watch our mothers getting ready. It's how we learn," I say. "Do you have a photo of her?" Jade pulls up a photo of her mom on her phone to show me. I can see how strongly she resembles her mother, especially with her high cheekbones and her lips.

Jade and I continue answering questions from the prompt deck and also take time between questions to get to know each other. I start to wonder if we have limitless time together and what will happen next. The experience is so curated yet allows for moments that feel organic. I notice my guard is a bit down just knowing we're in a virtual space. I really hate being touched and almost everyone forces a hug when I tell them my mom died.

Just as I'm starting to wonder this, we're interrupted.

"We invite you now to take some time and space away from the platform to process. Thank you for sharing, Bethany and Jade. We hope you enjoyed your time with each other," the same voice from before says.

A message pops up on the screen:

Take a break? Click YES to continue.

"You cool to take a break?" I ask Jade.

"Yeah, I need to get up and walk around a bit," she says. We both click "YES."

"Jade, it was so nice to meet you. I hope we can keep in touch," I say.

"We will!" she says, right as the screen turns off.

> **Bethany, we hope you enjoyed your conversation with Jade today.**
>
> **If you want to keep in touch with Jade, click Next.**
>
> **If you are not interested in speaking with Jade again, click Exit.**
>
> **If you aren't sure, click Not Sure and we'll keep Jade in your queue.**

I click Next.

> **Please share the way you would like to be contacted by Jade in the future.**
>
> **Remember, only share details that you are comfortable with.**

I add my email address to the form and click the submit button. I wonder if Jade will do the same. I think she will.

I log off the platform and decide to make myself some lunch. When I sit back down at my desk with a sandwich in hand, I notice I have a new email.

From: Jade
Subject: Egg Rolls

Hey Beth—it was really refreshing to meet you today. I hope we can talk again soon. I found some of those wonton wrappers in my fridge after we talked and was thinking... if you're ever ready to make egg rolls, we could do it together. Maybe it won't feel as scary.

-Jade

CHAPTER 13

INFLUENCER COACHES

In the year 2000, the Edelman Trust Barometer published the first of what would become an annual, global survey of the general public's responses to media, government, and business. In a 2019 report, they found 46 percent of consumers around the world do not trust traditional media. In addition, they found 63 percent of people trust what influencers say about products more than the brands themselves. A 2020 article published by Fashionable Data claims people today consume about eighty billion new pieces of clothing each year, a 400 percent increase from the early 2000s. They note this increase aligns perfectly with the rise of influencers.

Influencers play a massive role in what we do, say, buy, and support. Besides the wasteful nature of consumerism that comes with the territory, there is also a strict yet unspoken expectation to portray a lifestyle of perfection and ease. What would happen if influencers had more guidance and support in their toughest moments? Is there space for more genuine authenticity for those who already share intimate parts of their daily lives?

This piece introduces you to Marcie, who is presented with a new job opportunity as an influencer coach. Marcie's initial hesitance about the position is exacerbated by her conversation with her mom, whose opinions represent many people that tend to dismiss the profession of influencing. The tension in the story shows influencing is likely not going away anytime soon—and support for those who are creating the bulk of content on the Internet is necessary.

While influencer coaching is not a profession today, I hope this story sheds light on the back end of creating content for people while moving through difficult experiences.

It's 10 a.m. on a Tuesday morning. I shuffle through my PowerPoint slides one last time before I join my first meeting of the day. I stand in a Superwoman pose for five minutes each day before I start all of my meetings, hoping to jumpstart some sort of excitement my months of burnout simply can't access.

I'm just about to close my eyes and do a few breathing exercises when I notice a new direct message pop up on LinkedIn.

"Hi Marcie! We love the work you've been doing in DEI and think you'd be great for..." is all I can see in the preview.

I receive a ridiculously high volume of messages each day as a diversity, equity and inclusion consultant. Usually, the messages are from big businesses looking to absolve themselves of some guilt from malpractice or young professionals looking to follow in my footsteps. I normally book my lunch hour to sift through and see which messages are worth my while, but this one immediately catches my attention and I open it with just two minutes to spare before my presentation.

"Hi Marcie! We love the work you've been doing in DEI and think you'd be a great fit for our new Influencer Coaching Program! The increasing popularity of influencer careers through social media outlets has led us to create a six-month certification program that will lead itself into your own consulting career.

As an Influencer Coach (IC), you can continue scheduling your own hours and choosing your clients, but you have the opportunity to provide a more direct impact. We train coaches to teach on ethics, environmentalism, politics, emotional and physical wellness, and much more. We believe this work is a valuable solution to some of today's biggest problems, and we want you on our team! Check out our website and please follow up with any questions."

Well, that's a new one.

I close the message and make a mental note to return to it as I join my meeting. Today, it's with a group of young sales representatives. After introductions and a short icebreaker, I ask my first question. "Alright, who can tell me the difference between race and ethnicity?"

No answers. Lovely.

"Honey, you've been doing this for over ten years. Leaving would be a huge risk!" my mom tells me over the phone, after I tell her about the message I received a week prior.

"Well yeah, but so was leaving law school. So was starting this company! Make a better argument!" I joke.

"Well, I just don't get it. Why do we even need influencers anyways? Let's just get rid of 'em! I hate the superficial crap. You know, Karen just recently deleted all her socials. Said she's happier than ever!"

"Okay, boomer. That's not how this works. People aren't all just going to delete their 'socials' overnight. People make a living off this!"

"Alright so, what, you tell them what pictures to post and what lip injections to get next?" my mom asks. I can hear her chewing on carrots in the background. I hate when she does that.

"You're being so judgmental. And no, that's not at all what I'd be doing. It's a coaching program that influences ethics. It's everything I learned about in law school, just applied differently. I actually think I can make an impact," I say. Telling her this out loud makes me realize how much I've been fantasizing about this career switch since I read the message a week ago. Each day I visit their website and look for a reason against it, but the more I learn, the more interested I become.

"Aren't you making an impact now?" she asks me.

"No. Do you want to know what I got asked during a presentation last week? If I thought Simone Biles was faking it about having 'the twisties.'"

"God, yeah, people really don't change. Okay niña, you do what makes you happy. I'm just giving you a hard time," she says.

"As usual."

I hang up the phone and reopen the website from earlier.

I'm sitting at my desk, hanging up a post card I received from IC training that says "Consider the Impact" in bold lettering. I'm excited to start seeing clients and feel revved up from the training. Although it felt like the right move for me in my career, I decided to keep some of my contracting work on the back burner, just in case it's a total flop.

It's late in the morning before my first call. *Influencers really do work on a different schedule.*

I'm preparing and reviewing the materials for my first client. Her name is Deedee and she primarily posts lifestyle content on TikTok. Based on her following and the information I've been given, I see she is a microinfluencer. We learned about the distinctions between influencers and microinfluencers at training and I felt pulled toward the latter. A smaller audience can allow for more nuance in the influencer's reach and a more connected community.

Before I meet Deedee, I follow the protocols from training to help catch myself up to speed on her work. She hasn't seen an IC before and reached out to the program now that she has more followers and receives more offers for brand partnerships. The steps are as follows:

1. Scroll through your client's content and look at it objectively. How do you respond? Does it make you feel happy, content? Reflect and write down a reaction you can share with them.
2. Scroll through the content a second time and note the major themes of their content. Are they consistent?
3. Look at the brand partnership spreadsheet that has been shared with you. There are tabs for each category of brand (lifestyle, food, fitness, etc.). Cross reference these with our ethics app to consider the environmental impact of each organization and rate each partnership on a scale of one to five, one being least ethical.

This work is fun for me. It feels like there is a system and some protocols in place for this process. I like systems and protocols. I'm so caught up in organizing the spreadsheet from Deedee that I almost miss our first call together. I quickly hop on my computer and log onto our IC platform to video chat with her.

"Deedee! Hi, so nice to meet you. I'm Marcie, and we'll be working together for the next few weeks. How are you?" I ask. I can sense I'm a bit more nervous than usual when meeting new people and I can't quite pinpoint why.

"Hi Marcie. I'm excited to start working together. This is a huge relief—I've been in over my head with a lot of the back-end decisions of my content and I'm so glad to have some help. I hear you have a background in DEI, right?" she asks me.

"Yeah—yes. Mostly with larger corporations giving workshops and stuff to help them. It's hard, though. I'm excited to dive in here."

Ever the professional, I'm really used to drawing strong boundaries and keeping things moving. I can't tell if I'm being too abrupt, but I trust my instincts as a leader in the space. "I've taken a look at your content and it's really great. I think your aesthetic and consistency is a big reason why your following continues to increase and you're seeing more brand partnerships. Your content is relatively neutral as well, so it isn't likely to strike controversy. Is that intentional?"

"Yeah. I have to admit, I am a bit scared to share my opinions online. I derive a lot of my inspiration from more minimalist content, from people who show vlog-type content rather than more opinionated or activist pieces, I guess. It's not easy to receive criticism and I also want to respect the various communities that engage with what I share. I live in a predominantly White, suburban part of my state but as you'll see, my following is a blend of races, genders, and backgrounds," says Deedee.

I look at the chart I was sent that contains statistics about her followers and can confirm she does have a diverse group of people engaging with her work each day. I'm grateful this is the case because, from training, I have learned this is one of the harder issues to reverse once a creator has established themselves within one specific community.

Deedee and I go through some of her brand partnerships and talk about the environmental impact of each organization. We look into how the employees are compensated at the organization and I show Deedee how that compares to other salaries of similar nature. We balance that with the financial compensation for each advertisement and create a plan together for which partnerships she will accept and which ones she will decline.

As we continue speaking, I realize my nerves have calmed down. This feeling is familiar to me, reminding me of some of my first calls as a contractor in DEI. While I had all the training to back up the material I presented, I remember there was a learning curve of shaking off some of my imposter syndrome. I recognize that here, I also feel like an imposter to the realm of social media, which I barely use. But as we dive in more and more, I realize I understand Deedee's work and how we can make it better.

We're about to hang up when I notice a photo of a young man behind Deedee. He looks about her age.

"Is that your boyfriend?" I ask in an attempt to get to know each other a bit better. I'm usually a bit awkward at this, but I want to forge a relationship.

"Uh... no. That's my brother," she says. I can't figure out why her face has changed from the poise she's maintained during our call. "He died, actually. Yeah, he died last year," she says. As she shares these words, I can sense how unfamiliar they feel to her—like when you go to sit down in a place where a chair once was and fall. The memory is still there and the reality is hard to grasp.

"I'm so sorry, Deedee. What happened?" I ask.

"He... died by suicide. I don't really know how to talk about it, but yeah, I guess this was something I wanted to bring up. I'm sharing all this lifestyle content making smoothies and green juice and... when I'm done filming, I just throw it in the trash, and I get back into bed. I feel like I'm lying," she says.

"Is there anyone you talk to about this?"

"Yeah, I have my friends, and I'm in therapy too. But I feel really awkward bringing it up in my videos. I also feel like I'm lying by not bringing it up," she explains.

"Do you want people to know who he was?" I ask. I'm almost surprised by the question.

"Yes," she says immediately. "He was incredible. Everyone loved him," she tells me. I can see in her eyes she's looking back on memories of her brother.

Deedee and I spend the next twenty minutes talking about her brother, Ben. She tells me how he lit up a room, how funny he was, and how he somehow excelled at every class in college. At this point in my life, I've heard enough stories about people exactly like him leaving the world the way he did. It leaves a lump in my throat.

"I'm scared they'll judge him," she tells me when we circle back to our conversation about her social media pages.

I take a moment to sit with her words. I put myself in her position, as much as I can.

"You know what? They might. And they might judge you, too. But that really has nothing to do with you or him, does it?" I say.

I see her accept what I've said.

We discuss a few last-minute details about scheduling future calls and communications before we log off. I spend the rest of the day thinking about her and remembering the photo I saw of Ben.

I'm logging off a call with a new client I'm coaching, pondering some of their new brand deals, when I get a text from DeeDee.

"new post for approval, just sent to your email :)"

I've learned almost every influencer has chosen not to capitalize any of their words. It makes me laugh.

I go to my email and open a video from Deedee. She shows her morning routine, the usual products she uses to wash her face, and the outfit she puts on in the morning to begin journaling and going out for the day. As I watch, I listen to her words as she explains in a voice-over what she's doing, step by step. When she sits down to journal, I see the photo of her brother is precisely in the shot. I realize every other video of hers strategically avoided that angle.

"If you've made it this far, you might notice the photo in the background. That's my brother, Ben. He died last year. I'm not always sure how to talk to y'all about it, but as I'm recording my journal session, I just want to say that I'm writing about him today. It's officially one year since he passed, and I miss him all the time."

My eyes brim with tears as I watch her. I wonder what she's writing and about their relationship as siblings. I bet he would be proud of her.

When I finish the video, I message Deedee.

"I love it. I'm proud of you. Full approval on my end," I say.

"thanks" she texts back.

An hour later, I receive another text. It's a screenshot of the comment section.

tell us about your brother, if you want to

i lost my brother, too. i'm so sorry for your loss deedee.

we love you deedee

sending you strength

"thank you for encouraging me, marcie," Deedee messages me.

CHAPTER 14

@GOTTHEGRANDPAGENE

In February and early March of 2020, while on a work trip recording oral histories in the San Joaquin Valley, I was exposed to several stories of elderly LGBTQ+ people. These elders had been involved in some of the early creation of the acronym we now use: LGBTQ+.

They spoke of many themes, one of which was the HIV/AIDS epidemic and its removal of a generation of people who should be here with us today. I walked away from these conversations with a heavy heart and a deep appreciation for the work of those who have paved a better world for LGBTQ+ people now. My oral history brain also wondered: can we bridge gaps and keep this important history alive through intergenerational connections? What is the most accessible place for that to happen?

This story will introduce you to Grandpa Gene, an elderly gay man who recently lost his husband, Paul, to cancer. Gene, in his mourning, is introduced to social media where he can share about the memory of Paul and connect with LGBTQ+ youth. His story shows the ways social media can bridge generational gaps and open new avenues for community when we need it most and when we are unfamiliar with the idea of community at all.

I hum to myself while I put on a pot of water for tea. It's right around 5 p.m., the time my daughter calls me each day. I love to hear her voice, even if I know she's merely calling to check on me.

As the weeks pass, I've noticed more signs of spring coming—the earthy smell that lingers in my front lawn and the sound of children on my block playing outside after school. As the water boils for my tea, I sit at the kitchen table where I spend hours each day observing the birds who come to eat from my feeder, a gift from my granddaughter.

My phone begins to ring. *Right on schedule.*

"Hello darling," I say, with all the gusto I can muster for one sad old man.

"Hi Dad. How are you?" Cait asks me.

"Oh, the usual. Doing my puzzles, going to the center when I'm up for it," I say.

"Dad, I know you haven't been to the center in weeks. I just called them today," says Cait.

"She's caught me!" I joke. "I haven't been going, you're right. But I will, this week," I say to lighten the mood.

"Dad, why aren't you going? You used to love it there. I thought it was helping you with..." she trails off. I know what she's implying.

"Well darling, of course I love it there—it's where my friends are! But they all knew Paul. Sometimes I'd just prefer not to... Anyways, darling, tell me about *you*! How's the new job?" I've always been deft at deflecting from subjects I prefer to ignore. Cait hates it, but she plays along. I hate to hear the disappointment in her tone when I'm not doing great. We talk for a few more minutes and Cait asks if she can bring the kids over this weekend.

"They miss you! We don't see you as much since... you know. We'll bring lunch," she offers.

"Heavens, no. I'll fix something for us. See you then, sweetheart," I say.

I'm placing a tray of finger sandwiches on the dining table when I hear Cait's familiar duh-duh-duh knock at the front door. I place the last cucumber-and-mayo sandwich on its plate and wipe my hands.

"Come in!" I shout. The door opens with the sound of multiple pairs of feet walking into the house. Joanie and Devon, my grandchildren, gingerly walk over to me and give me big hugs. Cait follows behind with her usual load of tote bags full of things I don't need.

"Joanie! Your hair!" I exclaim as I look at her long, wavy curls that are now bright pink. I look up at Cait, who suppresses an eye roll.

"Yeah, I did it this week, all by myself!" Joanie says, the maturity of a thirty-year-old woman shining through her twelve-year-old self. "Here, I'll show you!" she says. Joanie motions for me to sit next to her on the couch while she pulls something up on her phone to show me. I swear these things are like another appendage of all kids these days. I pull my readers down from on top of my head and wait.

Joanie shows me a video. First, her hair is its natural blonde and then she's in the bathroom adding color to it and, voila—the final product appears, with some cheerful music in background.

"What a neat video! How did you do that?" I ask.

"TikTok! It's so fun, let me show you!" she says. Joanie presses a button and now I can see my face and her face on screen.

"Selfie!" I yell enthusiastically. The kids taught me this word a few years back. Sometimes I jokingly use that as my caption during the rare times I go on Facebook. Joanie and Devon burst into a fit of giggles afterward and Joanie plays the video back for me with a filter on it that turns my face into a dolphin when I open my mouth. It's so absurd, I can't stop laughing for two whole minutes.

"This is so silly! Is this what you do all day?" I say between laughter.

"Sometimes. But I actually make videos about other stuff. Here, I can show you," says Joanie.

As Cait and Devon help themselves to the spread of sandwiches, pastries, and jams on the dining room table, Joanie scrolls through what seems like an endless stream of videos. She's always been so great at hair and makeup, with a theatrical personality at that. I credit some of that to me and Paul, who always made a point of influencing the children with small touches of elegance and showing them the importance of outward appearances.

I find myself beaming with pride seeing her shine. "I want to watch these, Joanie! I'm so proud of you. Do you share these videos on Facebook too? That's all I do anymore," I say.

"No, but I can make you an account here. It's so easy, you'll love it! All you do is scroll and if you don't like something, just keep scrolling!" she says. I'm hesitant, but I hand over my phone, which has the most careful of all phone cases on it for my clumsiness. Joanie works on making an account for me, as she has done with my email and every other way I have to use these damn devices to talk to people anymore.

"Done!" she says, handing me the phone.

"Got the Grandpa Gene?" I ask when I see the page she's created for me under this name, @GottheGrandpaGene. It reminds me of the "Got Milk?" ads.

"Yeah, creative, huh?" she says with pride.

"As always. Okay, let's get off these damn devices and spend some time together," I say.

It's approaching dusk and I sit at my spot at the breakfast table where I eat my usual supper, a cup of soup and some tea. I watch as children ride bikes up and down the street, to the stop sign and back. I then look at the empty seat across from me, as I do each day.

I can tell my usual routine isn't going to work forever. My longing for Paul and the pit in my stomach linger each day. The sounds of children on the street, though cheerful, tend to remind me I have less and less in common with those around me. Their experiences of joy and delight bring me feelings of envy I wish I didn't feel.

I pick up my cell phone so I can go back and watch some of Joanie's videos; she is so creative and special. I watch her videos where she introduces herself to everyone, talks about her love for makeup, and shows how she does different looks she enjoys. It reminds me of back in my day, meeting Paul and helping him pick out a lovely outfit before we'd go to one of the underground gay bars in Los Angeles.

I love the way Joanie is so confident and shares who she is with the world. I wonder if I should try it. I click on the center button on the platform where I can record and decide to give it a try.

"Hello. My name is Gene, or Grandpa Gene, if you will. I am seventy-three years old. I have one daughter and two lovely grandchildren, one of whom made me this silly account." I pause briefly but press on. "Up until last December, I was married to the love of my life, Paul, for over thirty years. We were some of the first members of the LGBTQ community out here in Los Angeles when it formed—hell, we were here when it was just the 'G' community!" I give a small chuckle. "Paul was the light of my life. I miss him every day. I hope you all are being kind to one another and I hope you find love like I did. Take care now."

I finish and stop the recording, afterward clicking to post the video. I assume nobody will see it because Joanie said she is the only person who is subscribed to my page, but I know she'll like it. She loves when I talk about Paul—she loved him so dearly.

Something in me feels lighter after talking, just for that short amount of time. I don't always want to talk about Paul, but keeping his memory alive brings me strength. To reflect on our memories and the work we tried to accomplish back in our day brings me peace.

As I sip on my tea at my usual spot at the table, I embrace the silence of the warm spring morning. My thoughts are interrupted though, by the ringing of my phone. It's Joanie.

"Hello dearie, to what do I owe this pleasure? You never call!" I exclaim.

"Grandpa! You're famous!" says Joanie. "Did you see?"

"Heavens, no! What are you talking about?" I ask.

"TikTok! Your video about Paul! It has thousands of views. Grandpa, people love you. The comments are crazy—all these kids are asking you to be their grandpa too. They're LGBTQ and their families don't accept them," she says.

I'm in shock. I can't fathom so many people seeing my video. Thousands?

"Joanie, I have to go see for myself! How exciting!" I hang up my call with her and open TikTok. Just as she said, there are thousands of views and comments on my video. I begin to read through them.

So sorry for your loss Grandpa Gene we love you!

Thank you for telling us, RIP Paul.

Will you tell us about Paul?

What was Paul like?

My eyes well up with tears as I read these comments from complete strangers. I have to assume they are young, just like my Joanie. Their curiosity about Paul brings alive an emotion I haven't felt in eons and it reminds me of the curiosity I felt when I met him. I wanted to know everything—his favorite songs, favorite foods, and even the places he went to in his old neighborhood in the valley.

Ever since Paul died, I've noticed people's discomfort to bring him up. Cait, the kids, my friends at the center—it's as if they think bringing him up will make me cry on the spot. As if crying would be the worst response to losing him. I am caught off guard by the excitement of strangers who have never known him, wanting to uplift his life.

So, once again, I decide to record, and I tell the story of Paul: who he was before me and how we met. I set his story free and share him with the world.

And it feels wonderful.

CHAPTER 15

THE ROOM

Social media can often be an overwhelming flood of content that comes right at us whenever we use it. Like any other overwhelming or overstimulating experience, I believe this phenomenon blocks our ability to find connection with ourselves and each other.

The following story is meant to abstractly represent the way social media often feels like a fixed, unchanging space of sharing. It illustrates the complicated ways we interact intimately and yet at a distance with each other. This story represents how intention and slow change can impact the ways we share our lives with each other.

Imagine you walk into a room, unremarkable in size and decor. There is no furniture, with nothing to grasp onto but the people within it. You guess there are approximately a hundred people walking about and that they are all vibrant and beautiful. There are young people, elderly people, and everyone in between.

The first person you notice is a tall, beautiful woman in a sleek, black dress. You walk up to her, not sure what you're planning to say. She notices you and tells you where her dress is from. You nod politely and walk away.

You walk up to another woman. Her hair is pulled back and you can see that years of laughter have made wrinkles appear next to her eyes and around her mouth like parentheses.

"Riley learned how to walk today! We're so glad we were both there to see it! What a triumph!" she tells you.

"Uh... congrats!" you say. *Riley must be her child,* you think to yourself.

You're starting to get the hang of things now. You look around and choose who you'd like to approach next. You see someone who looks about your age, but they seem lost, vacant, really. You approach them and wait to be told information—where their shirt is from, what book is in their hand—but they say nothing. They just look at you.

"Hi," you say nervously.

"Hi," they say back. You can tell they are waiting for you to say something.

Should I tell them something? I'm not sure what to say.

The silence between you feels as if it has become eternal. Suddenly, like the emergent sensation of a ringing in your ears, you hear everyone's conversations all at once.

"Home renovations…"

"Well, we *love* this drink. We make it every week…"

"Is that polyester?"

"He only barks when we try to fall asleep…"

"I've never BEEN so in love!"

"I get this every day at the supermarket…"

"I love this song!"

"I hate this song."

"I love this show…"

"I hate this show!"

"I love this person!"

"I hate this person!"

"I'm Juniper," the person standing in front of you finally says. The noise stops. "Someone told me to come to The Room to help me recover."

"Recover?" you ask, but you're scared you shouldn't have asked.

"I was sick. But I'm here now. I hate The Room. Do you like it?"

"Er… I'm not sure. I guess so? Are there others—rooms, I mean?" you ask.

"Yes, they all look like this. They sound different sometimes, but they all look the same." As they say this, they pull a box of matches from their pocket. "I was thinking we could burn it down," they say, smirking.

"No!" you snap. "I just got here! I like it here! And there was someone I wanted to talk to, I just hadn't gotten there yet!" you say.

"You'll feel that way every day," they say.

You begin to feel frustrated at their matter of fact-ness.

"Well, have you ever tried changing The Room?" you ask. It feels so silly coming out of your mouth, you almost wish you hadn't said it.

"Be my guest," they say.

You turn toward the crowd and decide to scream at the top of your lungs. Nothing happens.

You look around the room again, searching for a microphone or a podium you might have missed at first glance. Nothing.

You turn toward Juniper, who is miraculously still there, looking at you as if you'll discover something new. You realize you were standing several feet apart this whole time, and you take three steps toward them. One more step and you begin to notice their dark brown eyes, the texture of their hair, and the small hoop in their bottom lip.

"Can I try something?" you ask.

They nod.

You reach your hand out and place it on their chest. They look at you, puzzled, but slowly stretch an arm toward your left shoulder.

You both look at each other, waiting for something to happen. Soon, you notice a small group of people surrounding you, observing.

"What's happening?" whispers Juniper.

"I think The Room changed," you say in awe.

CONCLUSION

It's early March of 2022 and I am walking around the Philadelphia Museum of Art. Outside it is a balmy and overcast day, perfect for meandering through hundreds of years of paintings, furniture, and artifacts. I follow my map into the modern art section and see a display called *Elegy: Lament in the Twentieth Century*.

Written on the back of the pamphlet I pick up is a short description of the work within: "*Elegy: Lament in the Twentieth Century* explores how artists have used their work to convey deep sorrow and commemorate those who have passed. Grief affects all of us, and mourning can take many forms."

The pamphlet is full of resources that have been compiled by a local group called the Philly Death Doula Collective. I had no idea one could be a professional death doula, but I learn their role is to "emotionally, physically, spiritually, and practically support end-of-life care for dying individuals and their families." Next to where I pull the pamphlet from is a bookshelf full of related fiction and nonfiction for people to read, placed behind two chairs where a young child sits.

I walk through the exhibit and see photographs and prints from funerals, depictions of the crucifixion of Jesus, and displays from Día de Los Muertos in México. I meander toward sculptures and see large faces representing Emmett Till and Martin Luther King Jr. I look at a large painting by Robert Motherwell, whose postdivorce grief led to a years-long project about the Spanish Civil War. The painting has large blob-like sections of black paint on top of grey areas. Its description suggests it evokes feelings of life and death for people because "the dark and light sections exist in complex dialogue."

This resonates.

In this exhibit, I am reminded of the complexity of the human experience. I am invited to connect to my own moments of grief as I look at the art in front of me. I am picturing the artists as they created their works, wondering if they worried about being misinterpreted or unseen in their expression.

I am also acutely aware that, in a large gallery, there is one space specifically dedicated to grief, full of diverse experiences and stories. It reflects that which is universal and terrifying, that which we are often afraid to know and be familiar with.

In an art gallery, you are expected to meander through the high-ceiling spaces with your hands behind your back, stopping to read and absorb. You are expected to be curious and make attempts to understand pieces even when they do not immediately make sense to you. There are guides to help you and books that interpret powerful work and its excellence.

Why do we lose that curiosity and willingness to understand when we leave these spaces? Why are we unwilling to connect with each other's expression in the same way?

On my way out of the *Elegy* exhibit, I snap a photo of the description of the collection within. This quote sticks with me:

"When the arts address grief, is their role to be cathartic, allowing the artists to express and viewers to feel intense emotion? Are they meant to be catalytic, instigating actions to rectify circumstances surrounding death that were unnecessary, unjust, and atrocious? Do the works offer some sense of commiseration and comfort? The goal of *Elegy* is to create a space for thinking about these powerful emotions and possible responses."

Elegy is the epiphany I was in search of for finding a clear through-line of my own work in this book. *For Crying Out Loud* is an invitation to think as well, but instead of an art gallery, we move into social media.

The artist and the viewer are both you, and we can learn from each other.

ACKNOWLEDGMENTS

I want to start off by thanking my parents, who gave me every tool they had so I could become the writer I am today. I am so proud to be your daughter. Thank you, Mom, for teaching me it's always a good time to dance and enjoy this one beautiful life we get. Thank you, Dad, for making sure I never take myself too seriously and reminding me that everything is always okay.

Thank you to my sister, Ashlyn, for constantly reminding me I need to trust my gut. For every reason you already know, I would not have been able to write any of this without you.

Thank you to all the storytellers who were willing to contribute their narrative to this book. Your stories mean so much to me and I think of them often. To my editors Mike and Michelle, thank you for bringing such patience and curiosity to what you do.

Thank you to the local coffee shops in Lancaster, Pennsylvania, mostly Prince Street Café. Thank you for providing me with the space to think and the caffeine to keep going.

Finally, thank you to the beautiful conglomeration of family, friends, and coworkers who make up the list below—thank you for supporting me in the earliest phases of this work. Whether you bought a copy, contributed time as a beta reader, or stepped up when I needed a reminder I can do this: you helped me tremendously.

Alan Jacks
Aleksandra Syniec
Alex Bushong
Alex Douglas-Deutsch
Alexandra Velazquez
Alexandria Combs
Alyssa Kray
Amber Morris
Andrea Bisbjerg
Anna Wagman
Annaliese Tucci
Anne McIlroy
Ashlyn Zikmund
Ava Ahmadbeigi
B. C. Fuge
Ben Simmons
Blak Wilson
Brandon Corbin
Brian Haig
Brittney Fatta
Brooke Miller
Brooke Pierce
Caleb Setlock
Caleb Yinger
Carlos Briceño

Carolina Marie Sguerra
Caroline Gabriele
Caroline Smiegal
Carolyn Goode
Carolyn Hoy
Carrita Thomas
Cheyne Thomas
Chris Caruso
Cindy McQuaid
Colby Weit
Connor Liu
Cynthia Smiegal
Daniel J Turner
Danielle Andersen
Danielle Melnick
Danielle White
Darwensi Clark
David Heckel
Diane Kay
Duanduan Hsieh
Eleanor Vassili
Elise Szabo
Elizabeth Sabatino
Ella Wiley
Emma Johnson

Emma Sullivan
Eric Koester
Erin Stroyan-Peduzzi
Eunice Cho
Evan Novacek
Gabrielle Glorioso
Gabrielle Spatz
Gavin G Schaffer
Hannah Guy
Hannah Smith
Harry Adams
Jacob Walker
Janel Brown
Jayson Szabo
Jenna Scotti
Jess Shober
Jessica Poje
Jill Glaser
Jodi Sweesy
Jonathan Zartman
Jonathan Zelinger
Jordan Barto
Jordan Roof
Julia Anne Martens
Julie Bushong
Kassidy Lesher
Katie Montgomery
Kayla J Gibbons
Kelly Larkin
Kelly Quinn
Kelsy Snavely
Keri Snyder

Kevin Zhu
Ki Jung
Kielan Prince
Kiernan Jordan
Killian Kueny
Kirsten Trauger
Kristen Claar
Lauren Stork
Lee Mottola
Lillian Karl
Lily Middleton
Lindsay Kelly
Logan Darling
Logan Hartlaub
Maddie Vouros
Madeline Spidel
Mande Bushong
Mary Jane Reynolds
MaryJo Viselli
Meg Hartman
Megan Sansevere
Megan Thiele
Michael Perezous
Michaela Williams
Nalani Saito
Nancy Zikmund
Natalie Cao
Natalie Saxon
Natasha Herring
Nate Nixdorf
Nick Beard
Nikki Dutta

Niomi Phillips
Nora Krantz
Olivia Bailey
Olivia Lyman
Patrice Turner
Patrick McNameeKing
Pauline Saternow
Perri Chinalai
Rachel Lapp
Rachel Mueller
Rachel Stern
Robyn L Zikmund
Ronald Zikmund
Ross Zikmund
Ryan McMahon
Ryan Woerner
Sandy Smith
Sara Nash
Sara Walbrecht
Sarah Matlock
Sarah Padgett
Shawn Cremer
Sonia Kinkhabwala
Steven Kressley
Susan E. Connolly
Taylor Ente
Taylor Stork
Teryon Lowery
Troy Smith
Whitney Smith
Wittney Ferguson
Zoë Kaminski

APPENDIX

INTRODUCTION

Abrahamson, Rachel Paula. "Why do people say such mean things about miscarriage and pregnancy loss?" *Today,* October 2020. https://www.today.com/parents/chrissy-teigen-pregnancy-loss-why-are-people-so-mean-t193054.

Dean, Brian. "Social Media Usage & Growth Statistics: How Many People Use Social Media in 2022?" *Backlinko,* October 2021. https://backlinko.com/social-media-users.

Molla, Rani. "Posting less, posting more, and tired of it all: How the pandemic has changed social media." *Vox,* March 1, 2021. https://www.vox.com/recode/22295131/social-media-use-pandemic-covid-19-instagram-tiktok.

Teigen, Chrissy. "Hi." *Chrissy Teigen* (blog). October 27, 2020. https://chrissyteigen.medium.com/hi-2e45e6faf764.

Teigen, Chrissy (@chrissyteigen). "We are shocked and in the kind of deep pain you only hear about, the kind of pain we've never felt before. We were never able to stop the bleeding and give our [...]" Instagram, September 30.

CHAPTER 1: THE SLOW TEMPERATURE CHANGE

Jeff Orlowski dir. *The Social Dilemma*. 2020; Boulder, CO: Exposure Labs. Malibu, CA: Argent Pictures. The Space Program. Netflix.

Lanier, Jaron. "How we need to remake the internet." Filmed April 2018 at TED2018, Vancouver. Video, 14:46. https://www.ted.com/talks/jaron_lanier_how_we_need_to_remake_the_internet.

Lanier, Jaron. *10 Arguments for Deleting Your Social Media Accounts Right Now*. London: Picador, 2019.

CHAPTER 2: CAN WE STOP PERFORMING?

Bo Burnham, Christopher Storer dir. *Bo Burnham: Make Happy*. 2016. Beverly Hills, CA: 3 Arts Entertainment. Netflix.

Jeff Orlowski dir. *The Social Dilemma*. 2020; Boulder, CO: Exposure Labs. Malibu, CA: Argent Pictures. The Space Program. Netflix.

Keating, Lydia. "I'm an influencer, and I think social media is toxic." *Slate*. February 1, 2022. https://slate.com/technology/2022/02/instagram-tiktok-influencer-social-media-dangers.html.

Santarossa, Sara and Sarah J. Woodruff. "#SocialMedia: Exploring the Relationship of Social Networking Sites on Body Image, Self-Esteem, and Eating Disorders." *Sage Journals* 3, no. 2 (2017). https://journals.sagepub.com/doi/full/10.1177/2056305117704407.

CHAPTER 3: OVERSHARING, OVERSHAMING

AARP, National Alliance for Caregiving. "Caregiving in the United States 2020." May 14 2020. https://www.aarp.org/ppi/info-2020/caregiving-in-the-united-states.html#:~:text=Today%2C%20more%20than%20one%20in,43.5%20million%20caregivers%20in%202015.

Blakemore, Erin. "Consciousness-Raising Groups and the Women's Movement." *JStor*. March 11, 2021. https://daily.jstor.org/consciousness-raising-groups-and-the-womens-movement/.

Cruz Kayne, Michael and Megan Neuringer. "Megan Neuringer." December 2, 2021. In *A Good Cry*. Produced by Headgum. Podcast, Spotify. 1:07:32. https://headgum.com/a-good-cry/megan-neuringer.

Cruz Kayne, Michael. "Michael Cruz Kayne." September 23, 2021. In *A Good Cry*. Produced by Headgum. Podcast, Spotify. 6:54. https://headgum.com/a-good-cry/michael-cruz-kayne#player.

Hannah Ritchie, Max Roser and Esteban Ortiz-Ospina "Suicide." *OurWorldInData.org*, 2015. https://ourworldindata.org/suicide#citation.

Heffernan, Lisa Endlich. "Oversharing: Why do we do it and how do we stop?" *Huffpost*. December 4 2013. https://www.huffpost.com/entry/oversharing-why-do-we-do-it-and-how-do-we-stop_b_4378997.

Krull, Erika, LMHP. "Grief by the Numbers: Facts and Statistics." *The Recovery Village*. May 26, 2022. https://www.therecoveryvillage.com/mental-health/grief/grief-statistics/.

Milano, Alyssa. "If you've been sexually harassed or assaulted write 'me too' as a reply to this tweet." *Twitter*. October 15, 2017. https://twitter.com/alyssa_milano/status/919659438700670976?lang=en.

Ohlheiser, Abby. "The woman behind 'Me Too' knew the power of the phrase when she created it—10 years ago." *Washington Post*. October 19, 2017. https://www.washingtonpost.com/news/the-intersect/wp/2017/10/19/the-woman-behind-me-too-knew-the-power-of-the-phrase-when-she-created-it-10-years-ago/.

CHAPTER 4: "HANDLING IT": INDIVIDUALISM AS THE ANTITHESIS TO COMMUNITY

Alger, Horatio Jr.. *Ragged Dick; and, Struggling Upward*. New York, NY. Penguin Books, 1985.

Health Resources & Services Administration. "Organ Donation Statistics." 2022. https://www.organdonor.gov/learn/organ-donation-statistics.

Kessler, David. *Finding Meaning: The Sixth Stage of Grief*. New York, NY. Simon & Schuster, Inc., 2019.

Lorde, Audre. *The Cancer Journals*. San Francisco. Aunt Lute Books, 1997.

The Free Dictionary by Farlex. "Horatio Alger Story." 2022. https://idioms.thefreedictionary.com/Horatio+Alger+story.

Worland, Justin. "Why loneliness might be the next big public health issue." *Time*. March 18, 2015. https://time.com/3747784/loneliness-mortality/.

CHAPTER 5: ALGORITHMS AND USER EXPERIENCES

Andrews, Mari. "Grief Baby." *Meta Bulletin*, February 13, 2022. https://mariandrew.bulletin.com/grief-baby/.

Bray, Bethany. "Helping clients develop a healthy relationship with social media." *Counseling Today*. September 24, 2020. https://ct.counseling.org/2020/09/helping-clients-develop-a-healthy-relationship-with-social-media/.

Demku, Amanda. "Instagram Adds New Chronological Views to Home Feed: Following and Favorites." *Later Blog*, March 23, 2022. https://later.com/blog/instagram-chronological-feed/.

Drain, Carson (@carryonwithcarson). "So the main question on my mind lately and I'm sure the minds of my friends and family are: 'hey Carson, why are you posting all this really personal stuff about [...]." Tik Tok, March 21, 2022. https://www.tiktok.com/t/ZTRec4F4t/?k=1.

CHAPTER 6: FINDING COMMUNITY

hooks, bell, 1952-2021. *All about Love: New Visions*. New York, NY. William Morrow, 2000.

Stern, Ken. "Episode 4: Generation Z and Caregiving." September 30, 2020. In *When I'm 64*. Produced by Standford Center of Longevity. Podcast, Spotify. 30:57. https://open.spotify.com/episode/4MfjwMdc3b9wtQJUvgJbi2?si=NdyQeqLxRYqqhjbdpKKA4g.

CHAPTER 7: WHEN WE HONOR THE LOVE, WE HONOR OURSELVES

Brown, Brené. "David Kessler and Brené on Grief and Finding Meaning." March 31, 2020. In *Unlocking Us*. Produced by Parcast. Spotify Original. Podcast, Spotify. 46:04. https://open.spotify.com/episode/02NfXb67kxDN55vNIURgPV?si=CkCFs-S3ITW2d6LctMP6ENA.

Kessler, David. *Finding Meaning: The Sixth Stage of Grief*. New York, NY. Simon & Schuster, Inc., 2019.

CHAPTER 8: HUMAN FIRST, PROFESSIONAL SECOND

London, Emily. "Comedian Laurie Kilmartin Tweets About Her Dying Father & It's Beautiful." *Refinery 29*, March 3, 2014. https://www.refinery29.com/en-us/2014/03/63514/laurie-kilmartin-live-tweeting-dads-death.

Murray, Holly. "What Simone's Step Back Teaches Us." *Athletes in Action*, July 30, 2021. https://athletesinaction.org/articles/what-simones-step-back-teaches-us/.

CHAPTER 9: SOCIAL MEDIA AS MODERN DAY MOURNING GEAR

Cruz Kayne, Michael and Caitlin Doughty. "Caitlin Doughty." January 20, 2022. In *A Good Cry*. Produced by Headgum.

Podcast, Spotify. 1:04:22. https://headgum.com/a-good-cry/caitlin-doughty.

McInerny, Nora. "We don't 'move on' from grief. We move forward with it." Filmed November 2018 at TEDWomen, Palm Springs, CA. Video, 14:51. https://www.ted.com/talks/nora_mcinerny_we_don_t_move_on_from_grief_we_move_forward_with_it?language=en.

Otto, Stacy. "A Garden from Ashes: The Post-9/11 Manhattan City-Shrine, the Triangle Fire Memorial March, and the Educative Value of Mourning." Journal of Social History 47, no. 3 (Spring 2014): 573-592. https://www.jstor.org/stable/43305950?mag=the-history-of-mourning-in-public&seq=6.

CHAPTER 10: BECOMING THE SPECTACLE: WHAT WE CAN LEARN FROM INTERACTING WITH GRIEF

Beppa (@grandpabeppa_). "I took a picture of my wife every time she looked beautiful this month." Tik Tok, February 4, 2022. https://www.tiktok.com/t/ZTRewBGMn/?k=1.

Brockes, Emma. "Performance artist Marina Abramović: 'I was ready to die'." *The Guardian*, May 12, 2014. https://www.theguardian.com/artanddesign/2014/may/12/marina-abramovic-ready-to-die-serpentine-gallery-512-hours.

Marina Abramovic Institute. "Marina Abromovic on performing 'Rhythm 0' (1974)." March 5, 2016. Video, 3:07. https://www.youtube.com/watch?v=xTBkbseXfOQ.

Suede Brooks (@suedebrooks). "Lost my father very sudden a few months ago." Tik Tok, December 10, 2021. https://www.tiktok.com/t/ZTRewDCxk/?k=1.

CHAPTER 12: INFLUENCER THERAPIST

Thornton, Brett. "From an 'Accidental Influencer' to an SVP, Alex Vailas Breaks it All Down." *The Fam*, August 18, 2021. https://

fam.news/from-an-accidental-influencer-to-an-svp-alex-vailas-breaks-it-all-down/.

CHAPTER 14: INFLUENCER COACHES

Da Silva, Lauren. "How Influencer Culture is a Sustainable Disaster." *Fashionable Data*, June 15, 2020. https://www.fashionabledata.com/blog/how-influencer-culture-is-a-sustainable-disaster.

Falls, Jason. "Why Consumers Care About Influencers, and Why You Should Too." *Entrepreneur*, February 10, 2021. https://www.entrepreneur.com/article/364993.

CONCLUSION

Elegy: Lament in the 20th Century. Philadelphia Museum of Art, Philadelphia. https://philamuseum.org/calendar/exhibition/elegy-lament-20th-century.

www.ingramcontent.com/pod-product-compliance
Lightning Source LLC
LaVergne TN
LVHW012018060526
838201LV00061B/4364